The Five-Year Voyage

Exploring Latin American Coasts and Rivers

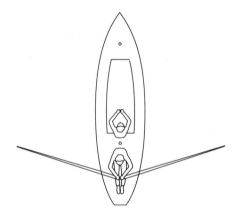

by Stephen G. Ladd

Seekers Press

Ladd, Stephen G.
The Five-Year Voyage: Exploring Latin American Coasts and Rivers
ISBN: 978-0-9669337-1-0
Library of Congress Control Number: 2021903105
Dewey Decimal 910.45 (Ocean voyages)

Published by:
   Seekers Press
   938 E. 31st Street
   Bremerton, WA 98310
   To order a copy transmit $20 (includes shipping and tax)

Cover by Mykola Gorielov and Donika Mishineva
Photographs by Virginia Ladd
Maps by Stephen Ladd
Manufactured in the United States of America

10 9 8 7 6 5 4 3 2 1

CONTENTS

MAPS

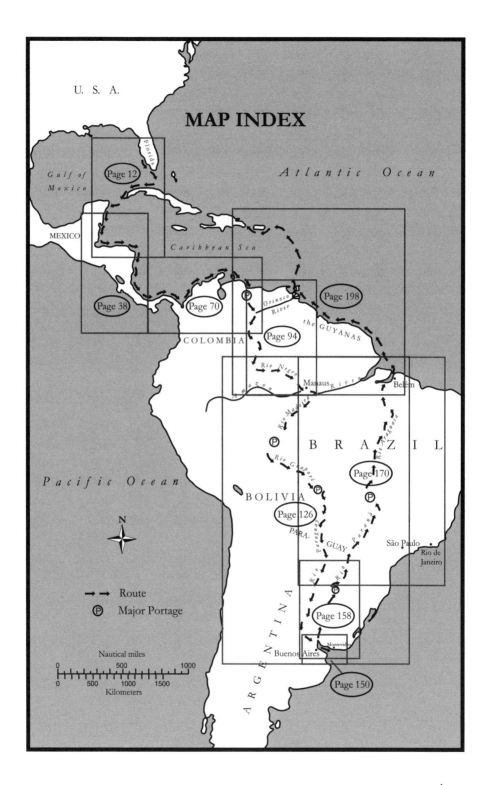

MAP INDEX

U. S. A.

Atlantic Ocean

Gulf of Mexico

Florida

Page 12

MEXICO

Caribbean Sea

Page 38

Page 70

Page 198

Orinoco River

Page 94

the GUYANAS

COLOMBIA

Rio Negro

Manaus

River

Belém

Amazon

Rio Madeira

Rio Araguaia

B R A Z I L

Rio Guaporé

Page 170

Pacific Ocean

BOLIVIA

Page 126

N

PARA-

GUAY

Paraguay

Paraná

São Paulo

Rio de Janeiro

Rio

Rio

Page 158

A R G E N T I N A

Montevideo

Buenos Aires

Page 150

→ ► Route

Ⓟ Major Portage

Nautical miles

0   500   1000

0   500   1000   1500

Kilometers

FOREWORD

I first met Steve at a wooden boat festival when he was selling his earlier book, *Three Years in a Twelve-Foot Boat*. I thought something like, "The crazy things people do!" But I was intrigued. In subsequent years I got to know him, and now I am honored to be asked to provide this foreword for a book on a subsequent voyage.

So you know, I have been a Coast Guardsman, fisherman, shipwright, marine surveyor, charter skipper, and delivery skipper. In my wooden sailboats I have gone places simply for the adventure of it, too. I know the waters from Mexico to Alaska.

For years I bought fish from the Yu'pik Indians on the Kukoskwim River, which flows into the Bering Sea. The Kukoskwim wasn't as big as the monstrous rivers Steve and Ginny explored in South America. And I never got above tidal range, maybe ninety miles up, whereas they went right up into the headwaters. But I had my challenges too, like entire days of steering through snowstorms and hail storms with nothing to see but the shadows on my radar screen.

My working seasons were long and the distances were great, but they lacked the huge scope of Steve and Ginny's voyage. Their travels were so unusual and extensive! It'd be easier to go around the world a couple of times than to do what they did. Compared to modern, ordinary living they took risks that were almost unimaginable.

I've been around boats and small ships all my life, but I haven't much experience with ultra-light craft like what Steve uses. Their vessel of choice was tiny compared to the deep-draft boats you mostly see. I find ultra-small boats interesting, though I don't particularly recommend them myself. Personally I like a larger vessel under me.

Still, they chose a boat that was appropriate for the job, then modified it to suit their needs to a tee. The pictures depict *Thurston* quite clearly. Her small size and shallow draft required a specialized expertise, but Steve explains technical matters well, so I easily grasped his methods. His boat handling in all these conditions showed extreme skill. I appreciated that a lot. And his accounts of the native boats and how they were used wherever they went were also very interesting. From local watermen they were able to gather information useful to them regarding their route ahead.

Basically, Steve and Ginny went from Florida to South America following coasts and islands, then they got into those big river systems down there. Using those rivers they went up and over a big hump called the Guyana Massif, which is the highland between the Orinoco and Amazon watersheds. Then they went up and over another big hump: the high ground south of the Amazon and north of Argentina. They had their baby down past that second hump, where South America tapers off and gets narrow. Then they crossed that second hump again, coming back northwards into the Amazon, but following different rivers this time. When you look at it on a map you see they did a lot of switch-backing, because the streams may have an overall direction but they zig and zag a lot, too.

The tales of saltwater sailing are great, but their river travels were truly unique. A river is a place of powerful and changing currents. They demonstrated a lot of skill in that. As they went upstream they would eventually get above the limit of tidal rises and falls. Then they still might have thousands of miles to go! Going up, the river would get smaller and smaller as they got themselves above where the various tributaries feed in. Eventually it was nothing but a creek. When it was no longer navigable even in their tiny boat they found a way to transport it to a stream flowing downhill on the other side. Then the process went in reverse, with it getting larger and larger as tributaries came in. Then they would come out some estuary of gigantic proportions.

Just as tides add a vertical dimension, so does seasonal variation in rainfall. They caught a period of record high flooding on the Amazon and its tributaries. They must have been going over small islands and farmland a lot of the time there! It boggles the mind to think of rivers so big you can't see land on the other side. Then they sailed through that Mato Grosso swamp that's like the size of the State of Washington! Who does that? I was very impressed. And the things they noticed and described along the way I found interesting too, from Indian hieroglyphics to huge cities surrounded by jungle, that you can only get to by water or air. They ranged back and forth between remote wilderness and dense, third-world cities.

Like me in my travels they sailed when they could and motored the rest of the time. But their motor was way smaller than anything I used. In fact, the Honda two-horse outboard is probably the smallest motor on the market anywhere. They finally wore it out, ruining its tiny single cylinder. But they eventually found a backyard mechanic who was able to get it going again. This points out the commendable way in which they dealt with languages, cultures, clearances and permissions.

Ladd brings all this out with a great quality of description. He is clear and concise about geography, weather, river state, and the people. And he intersperses it with endearing personal scenes of his and Ginny's life together, right down to how they coordinated their tooth brushing! They had to get along, and they really did. It was a mutual adventure and they helped each other all the way. You could tell they consistently enjoyed the simple pleasures of their life together. Finding a compatible female partner aboard a vessel can be hard, and Ginny was exceptionally brave and adaptable. Her photographs are really good, too. They add a lot.

This is a book about entire watersheds. It's about the largest rivers in the world, from their first trickling starts to their sprawling deltas. And it's about the coastal and ocean travel required to get there and back. Actually, their boat *didn't* make it back. Steve lost it in surf in the Dominican Republic. Thankfully they all survived and have produced this book for us. I would recommend it to any small boat sailor who dreams of big adventure.

James "Captain Jim" Peacock
Chimacum, Washington
April, 2021

PREFACE

Ginny and I were equal partners in this voyage and book. We both kept journals. Drawing from them I periodically drafted travelogues. Ginny proofread them, incorporated her photos, and emailed them to friends and family. We also published these travelogues as "The Adventures of Ginny and Steve," at ginnyandsteve.blogspot.com. (Go there for the full-color versions of the photographs on these pages, and many others besides.) Using the blog as a starting point we created articles for Small Craft Advisor magazine. They published them in their issues #66 through #95, every two months for five years. This book draws from all the above materials.

If you've read *Three Years in a Twelve-Foot Boat* you will recognize me as the author, but my voice is different here because Ginny is with me. My emotions are more stable and my viewpoint is augmented by hers. Gone are the poems, added are the photos. Ginny and I are incredibly lucky to have found, in each other, a thoroughly compatible partner in adventure. We being two, difficult things were easier and funny things were funnier. Curiosity and love fueled this voyage.

This story's drama stems not from our relationship but from the challenging nature of the voyage. It was fully as ambitious as that narrated in *Three Years in a Twelve-Foot Boat*. We traveled much further, through lands even more remote, but with a small motor most of the time. Our extensive navigation in the interior rivers of South America, from Venezuela south to Uruguay, then north to the mouth of the Amazon at Belém, is particularly unique.

My favorite subjects have always been history and geography. You will find some history here, such as about the early European explorers along our route, and the new people types (Garafunas, gauchos, etc.) that resulted from the conquest. You will find *a lot* of little-known geography. Thus we include nine maps plus an Index thereof. Throughout we have striven for accuracy, right down to the Portuguese diacritical marks which one must use to properly spell delightful place names like Maurilândia.

Thank you to everyone who facilitated us, especially Ginny's mother, Lois, our friends Larry and Karen Whited, Josh Colvin of the Small Craft Advisor, and the new-made friends who helped us along the way. The latter are part of this story.

Stephen Ladd
Bremerton, Washington
May, 2021

Chapter 1
AN IDEA THAT WOULD GROW

My earlier book, *Three Years in a 12-Foot Boat,* occupied the years 1990-93. Subsequently I worked again as a city planner in the Puget Sound region. Ginny and I met as fellow employees of the City of Bonney Lake, where she handled the City's records and web site. Our dates were all hikes, bike rides, and canoe trips. When winter came we bought snow shoes and continued our weekend outings. Her wanderlust and love of nature matched my own! We fell in love dreaming of the adventures we could have together.

In 2007 the dam burst. We quit our jobs, jumped into my Isuzu pickup with a canopy on back and a canoe on top, and snorkeled the Caribbean coast of Mexico and Belize for six months. But the canoe couldn't get us to the outer reefs, where the water was especially clear, so we contemplated a bigger boat. Thus was born the idea for this voyage. It would slowly grow into something much larger.

Ginny hadn't sailed before, but she was brave, hardy, and non-materialistic. I had designed my twelve-footer, *Squeak.* She was sail- and oar-powered. She had a cabin big enough for one and was seaworthy enough for coastal and inter-island sailing. To save time Ginny and I decided to look for a used boat with comparable sea-worthiness but big enough for two. It was unlikely a boat that size could be dragged up a beach unaided, like *Squeak,* but she should be light enough to row if we gave her a sliding seat to harness the strength of our legs. We had fun traveling around the country looking at used boats. Then we saw a 1985 Sea Pearl for sale in Panama City, Florida. We fell in love with her!

She was based on a design by L. Francis Herreshoff and manu-factured by Marine Concepts of Tarpon Springs, Florida. She was twenty-one feet long on deck. Her draft was only six inches, her weight only six hundred pounds. Her cat-ketch rig and leeboards looked simple and effective. She was in good shape and unmodified. We bought her in November, 2008, for $3,000 and moved her to Larry and Karen Whited's house near Atlanta. I had met Larry through an on-line fo-rum he hosted about Sea Pearls. Ginny and I joined their household and put his boat shop to work. Thank you again, Larry and Karen, for helping our dream to come true!

In an early trial she capsized in a sudden gust. The Sea Pearl is an open boat, so she filled with water and stayed afloat only due to her flotation. Other boats rescued us, but the episode underscored the need to add a cabin top over the hold, or central cavity of the boat. The opening was seven feet long and three feet wide. We built a male mold then constructed the top using 3/8" by 3/4" cedar strips, a pro-cess called strip-planking.

Building the cabin top

We covered it with fiberglass, added a bottom flange, and attached it over the opening with twenty-seven #10 bolts. The top had a hatch at its aft end and three portholes. I capsized the boat again, this time intentionally. No water entered. She floated high on her side, allowing me to right her by standing on a gunwale and leaning backward, pulling on a line attached to the opposite side of the boat.

The cabin proved successful as a bedroom, too. The roof was tall enough to sit up in "bed," the latter being the entire floor of the cabin, which was eight feet long and three feet wide on average. We found it best to sleep with our heads at opposite corners and lay diagonal to each other, with a mosquito net over the hatchway.

The Sea Pearl has a bit of rocker but is flat-bottomed transversely. That allowed us to build a system of water tanks and storage bins running the width of the boat. We had them made out of heavy aluminum tubing 4"x4" in section. There were twelve tanks and twelve bins. The only difference between them was that the tanks had necks at one end in which we fitted strong-sealing plugs, while the bins were

Fitting tanks and bins

mostly cut away on their upper surface. They were short forward, where the boat was narrower, and got longer aft as the boat got wider. They all lay side by side flat on the bottom.

Then we added aluminum floor boards to hold the tanks and bins down in the event of capsize. The floorboards were capped on each side by rail-like structures. These gave enough clearance to slide one floorboard up and over another to gain access to a set of tanks or bins. To open the floorboards we had to move aside one or more of the fitted cushions we created to serve as a mattress. Total tankage was eighteen gallons. The weight of our water and bins made our boat much more stable. My accordion added a little weight too. We secured it aft of the mainmast step and forward of the floorboards.

The Sea Pearl has a roomy aft cockpit. Here we installed a sliding seat rowing station equipped with nine-foot oars. After much tinkering we ended up with an ergonomic system that we could rapidly put in place or stow out of the way. We installed steering lines so one of us could steer facing forward while the other rowed facing aft. We found that we could row the boat at a steady 2.5 knots in flat conditions.

We next built a sealed storage compartment at the stern of the boat. We called this the lazarette. Everything we needed during the day was easily accessible there. The lazarette nicely complemented the cabin top, being of the same materials and crown curvature.

Our headlamps, camera, running lights, GPS, and VHF would all run on disposable batteries, so we didn't need much of an electrical system. We installed a twenty-watt solar panel on the cabin top and a twelve-volt, 10.5 amp-hour battery at the base of the main mast. These sufficed to charge our laptop, cell phone, and Kindles and still enjoy an episode of The Simpsons at the end of the day.

The Sea Pearl has two masts of equal height. They fit into sockets. To hold them up horizontally when not in use we made holders that fit into the same sockets. The holders held the masts side by side, about four feet above the cockpit floor. Now we could row without the windage of the masts. We could also drape a big awning over the masts and hook its edges onto the gunwales. The awning would prove indispensable in sun and rain. After painting the boat we christened her *Thurston* after a cat of Ginny's that passed away during that time. As the cat was noble and perfect, we hoped the boat would be also.

High on Ginny's curriculum vitae is that at an early age she mastered Tetris, the game where things have to be packed tightly together. What luck, because *Thurston* didn't have much volume! Ginny took the lead in installing shelves and holders. Cooking with our white gas stove and 1.5-liter pressure cooker we could be self-sufficient for two weeks at a time. We didn't have refrigeration, so she stowed fruits and vegetables in a net under a side deck. The cost of all this compactness was what we called our "take outs and put aways." Whenever one of us was in the cockpit and the other was in the cabin, the former could rightfully utter the words, "Take outs and put aways!" The person inside then had to get things out and put things away. This required varied contortions depending on where the item was located. Objects under the cockpit were the worst, being accessed only from the cabin through a very constricted space. It was like crawling under a sports car without the benefit of a jack except that there was also an obstacle in the middle: the mizzen mast step. Everything forward of the desired object had to be removed before you could reach what you wanted. We only put things rarely needed back there.

By December, 2009, we were the proud owners of a safe, fast, minimal, long-distance cruiser for two.

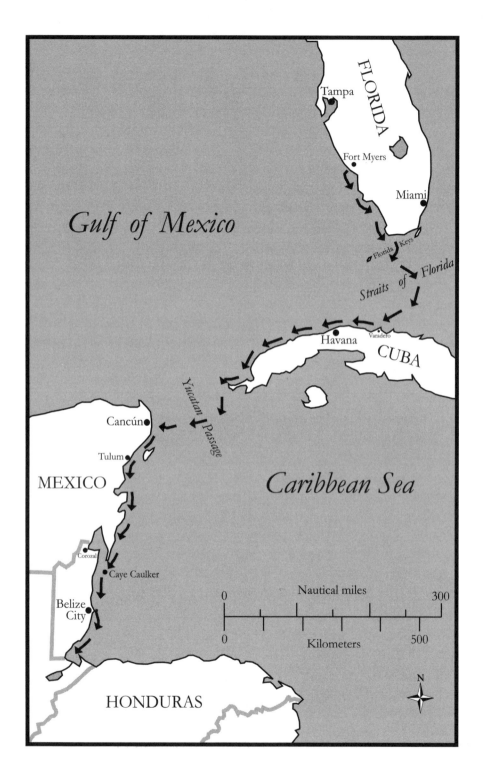

Chapter 2
SOUTH TO THE REEFS

When our boat was ready we towed her down to Pine Island, Florida, on the gulf coast near Fort Meyers. We had arranged to leave our truck and trailer there. We planned to spend the winter cruising south, then return to Larry's in the spring for debugging if necessary. On December 19, 2009 we launched in shallow Pine Island Sound.

Launching in Pine Island, Florida

With *Thurston* looking and feeling great we sailed over to Captiva Island and tied up in a mangrove lagoon. Her shallow draft allowed us to come in close and wade ashore. Emerging from a thicket we found ourselves in the middle of a swanky resort! Our legs were covered with mud and our hair was full of sticks, but no one seemed to notice as we stretched our legs. Curiosity satisfied, we returned to our hideout and slept well this first night of our voyage. This life definitely suited us!

The days were short, so we typically rowed or sailed only about fifteen miles per day and spent the night where we could "parallel park" at a beach sheltered from waves. To do this we situated the boat a few feet from shore and parallel to it. We then set one anchor forward and the other astern, tying them off with hardly any slack. Then we tied a third line to something on land. To get ashore we just pulled on this line until we could step out onto land. When we let go the tension between the two anchors caused *Thurston* to sidle back into place.

We spent Christmas in ritzy Marco Island, where we did some minor boat refitting. The only suitable parallel-park anchorage was across a narrow channel from a lofty condo building. One afternoon it started raining hard. We got in the cabin. Then I said, "Why waste fresh water? I'm taking a bath!" I plugged the drain and waited for water to rise in the cockpit. Then I took a bath with my swim suit on. I had just put my clothes back on when a County sheriff boat pulled alongside. He checked our documents and safety equipment, asked how we handle sewage, and wrote up a report. He suggested another place to anchor, then departed. We got the message. Somebody up in one of those apartments had called the cops on us for being aquatic hobos! Oh well, we were ready to go anyway.

Continuing south we entered the Ten Thousand Islands, where the Everglades transition into mangrove islands. For nearly two weeks we camped on uninhabited Panther Key. It has some beach around its edges but is mostly mangrove. We arrived several days early for a gathering of the West Coast Trailer Sailors. We anchored in a tiny lagoon that drained and refilled with the tide. It was a good place to make further boat improvements, such as an improved pair of oar rests. We set up the tent on the beach and had a campfire going when our fellow sailors got there. Unfortunately, their arrival coincided with record low temperatures and high winds. The thermometer dropped below freezing. Thousands of dead fish lined the shore, killed by the cold! The other sailors left. We stayed on, merely surviving. We scavenged old clothes and pillows from an abandoned campsite and wore everything we had. For two days we barely left the tent. We weren't prepared for "Arctic in the Everglades!"

On Panther Key.
The Sea Pearl's flat-ish bottom allows "drying out,"
also known as sitting "on the hard."

We bought provisions at Everglades City then spent a week skirting the Everglades National Park. We camped at Pavilion Key, Graveyard Creek, and the Little Snake River, rarely seeing other people. Sometimes there was a bit of shore on which to stretch our legs. Other times our anchorage was only a patch of open water surrounded by dark mangrove trees, the lower stratum of which is a thick tangle of roots dipping into muddy shallows.

Strong south winds pinned us down in the vicinity of Cape Sable. After beating to windward one day we discovered a gallon or two of salt water in the cabin. *Thurston* had no bilge for water to pool up in, so we painstakingly removed the tanks and bins, mopped up the water, and fixed the leak, which was in a mast step. Next our water tank caps started coming loose. After again dismantling everything and mopping up we secured the caps with Velcro straps.

In the muddy mangroves of Cape Sable

SOUTH . . .

The winds in south Florida usually shift clockwise. When the south wind veered west we tried to round Cape Sable again. Just as we breasted the promontory the northern horizon became black. The sea turned a sickly yellow-green, dully illuminated from the fading rays of the sun. Lightning crackled. "I'm scared," said Ginny. Then the black cold front rolled over us. The wind shifted to north. Rain beat down, blinding us and whipping the sea into a lather. Ginny bailed. "Why don't you just pull the cockpit plug?" I asked. "I need to do something to keep from freaking out!" she said.

It didn't last long. The cleansed wind sped us to the Everglades National Park headquarters at Flamingo. There we anchored next to real land and hiked the Coastal Prairie Trail, relishing the chance to walk, smell land, and experience strange new ecosystems.

Florida Bay is like an armpit in that it lies between the Florida mainland (the torso) and the Keys (the arm) and it's "hairy" with lots of wispy mangrove shoals. We were advised to sail south around it, but we figured that if any boat can tackle Florida Bay it's a Sea Pearl. We cut straight through the middle, seeking out channels and navigating through far-flung islets. The water became clear, the bottom covered with turtle grass. We ran aground, got out into the thin muck, and pushed her to deeper water. Other times we had to back up and find a different channel. At dusk we grounded yet again. This time the tide was dropping so we called it a day. The lights of the Keys shone in the distance. The water around us was ankle-deep but the bottom didn't support weight. We cooked a meal and slept peacefully, the hatch open. No bugs out here! At high tide I rowed us beyond that shallow patch, re-anchored, and went back to sleep.

In the morning we landed on Plantation Key. This and several other islands make up a city called Islamorada. Anchoring where we could wade ashore, we re-provisioned and started rebuilding our attachment points for securing anchors and rodes to the foredeck, the originals having fallen apart. "Always the boat work," grumbled Ginny.

On the third day a gentleman on shore yelled out that it was illegal for us to be there, so we relocated to Upper Matecombe Key. This time we lowered the masts and tucked under some mangrove branches where we could wade to a public street end. We took the bus to various stores. The foam in our cushions had gone flat already so we replaced it with heavier foam. We installed brackets for mounting a stern light and created little cardboard-and-epoxy shelves in the four corners of the cabin to hold small items that would otherwise get lost.

This new location worked for two weeks, but we were still in Islamorada, and the local cops were onto us. They came by every day asking unfriendly questions. They admitted we weren't breaking any laws. We weren't tied to the mangroves. *Thurston* was too short to require a holding tank. I hadn't bathed in the cockpit. Other live-aboards were anchored all over the place. But someone had complained specifically about us because we were much closer to shore than the other boat bums. Upstanding citizens were feeling hemmed in by ne'er-do-wells. The cops demanded we anchor further out, but we didn't have a dinghy, so we fled again.

Determined to finish a project before continuing down the Keys we moved to a forgotten canal surrounded by trees on the ocean side of Windlay Key. This time we built a strange apparatus on the forward surface of the lazarette. It was a combination footrest (the original one having been in the wrong position) and garbage bin. Whenever we emerged from the woods onto the public road we were careful to not be seen.

After three weeks in hobo-hating Islamorada we sailed to Marathon, the next town down the chain of islands. In its center is Boot Key Harbor where hundreds of boats lie anchored and moored. The live-aboards were a tight community with a daily 9:00 a.m. chat on VHF radio. Many had been there for years. We made friends with boaters from New Brunswick, Ohio, and Ontario. One of them gave us an inflatable dinghy, solving the problem of how to get ashore. It was a hassle making room for it on the boat, but when you need a dinghy you really need one. Marathon was even better than Islamorada for doing boat projects. A West Marine, Home Depot, Publix, and K-Mart were all within walking distance. We added a new pair of shelves, spice racks, and little longitudinal bulkheads under the cockpit to facilitate stowage.

Thurston was pretty well debugged. It wasn't necessary to return to Larry's house in Georgia before proceeding to the Caribbean. The truck and trailer were okay where they were. The weather was finally warm enough for T-shirts, but the water was still too cold to swim.

South, always south! Unfortunately our route to the Yucatán and Belize could no longer be coastal; a sea passage would be necessary. From the southwest tip of the Florida Keys to the Yucatán is 290 nautical miles, way too far! (In this book "miles" will always mean nautical miles if we're talking about water. A nautical mile is 1.15 statute miles.) The only way to get to the Yucatán in smaller hops would be via the north coast of Cuba. For that, Marathon would be a good point of departure.

The U.S. then had a trade embargo against Cuba but you could go there for professional reasons, such as journalism, under a "general license." We were writing articles on the voyage for publication by *Small Craft Advisor*, a magazine. Arguably this made us journalists. We decided to proceed on that basis, but there was another legal hazard. Due to a "National Marine Security Emergency" you couldn't sail from the U.S. to Cuba without a permit that was pretty much impossible to get. The wording implied, however, that by sailing from the U.S. to the Bahamas, then to Cuba, we would circumvent the do-not-cross zone. In my 1993 return from Cuba I had stopped over at tiny Sal Cay, which is on the edge of a vast bank quite separate from the other Bahamas. That would be our stopover this time too.

The knowledge that we were heading out to sea seemed surreal, nerve-wracking yet exhilarating, especially to inexperienced Ginny. In the wee hours of our departure date the houseboat next to us caught fire. It burned like a torch all night. By dawn it was all gone except some charred, half-sunken remains. On that somber note we hauled in our anchors and left Marathon.

At 6:00 p.m. we entered the Straits of Florida. A northwest wind was blowing at ten to fifteen knots. The sun set. No moon or stars. The blackness made our speed seem much greater and our motion more violent. We couldn't see the waves to brace against them, and we had the Gulf Stream to worry about. Our goal lay to the southeast, but the current flows northeast. Our GPS track showed that the current was flowing about as fast as we were sailing, so by sailing southeast we actually went east. We steered south to compensate, which drastically reduced our speed-made-good. We should have cut straight across and made up the difference later. It's like swimming across a river: you have to go straight across and not worry about being swept downstream. Time went by incredibly slowly. We traded off taking little naps curled up in the cockpit and yearned for daylight.

As dawn broke the wind died. The ocean was empty. Two conflicting patterns of swells furrowed its gray surface. I set up the rowing station, but the wind soon returned. Around noon our track showed that we had finally escaped the Gulf Stream. We sailed through a broken perimeter of sharp rocks against which the sea bashed, called Dead Man Rocks! Inside was Sal Cay Bank. The water was turquoise, thirty feet deep. Sal Cay lay twenty-five miles southwest across that bank. We sailed fast all afternoon, anxious to avoid a night landfall. At sunset we entered Sal Cay's lee and anchored in crystal clear water. It was as remote and lovely as in 1993. We still had half the distance to go. Cuba lay thirty miles south, then we had to travel fifty-five miles west along the coast to get to a port of entry, the resort town of Varadero.

The following day we sailed south. At dusk, upon glimpsing a Cuban lighthouse beacon, we turned west. To avoid entering their territorial waters prematurely we kept five to ten miles from land all night.

The Sea Pearl reefs by rotating the mast in its socket, thus wrapping the sail around the mast. It's a good thing this is an easy procedure because she is a tippy boat, requiring frequent adjustments to sail area. We already had several wraps in both main and mizzen when, at 10:00 p.m., the wind increased alarmingly and veered from north to northeast. We tightened the mizzen sheet and loosed the mainsheet. She pointed into the wind; mainsail flapping. I clipped my harness to a tether, inched forward while gripping the handholds on top of the cabin, and reefed the main until only a small triangle remained. We brought *Thurston* back on course, now with the main to one side, the mizzen to the other ("wing-on-wing"). Our speed was still a good four knots. As Thurston rolled and pitched we braced ourselves and again wished we had stars to steer by. We passed another endless night.

Finally we started seeing the lights of Varadero, where tourist hotels line the beach for ten miles. I donned a Cuba T-shirt I had been saving for this moment. We already had the quarantine flag up. At dawn we turned landward, entered a narrow channel with surf crashing on either side, and tied up at a small marina. Safe!

For two hours we underwent formalities with various officials, then were free to wander. The marina harbored a dozen yachts, mostly Canadian. Our fellow sailors starting filling us in. Everything was strange! There were two currency systems. The *peso convertible* bought you manufactured goods and luxuries like international phone calls. The prices were so-so for someone exchanging U.S. dollars. The *peso de moneda nacional* bought fruits and vegetables from farmers' markets, bread from *panaderias*, and street food. Anything bought with *moneda nacional* was ridiculously cheap, but such outlets were hard to find and they were often closed due to shortages. Many goods couldn't be bought with any currency. No one seemed to sell writing paper or building materials, for example.

Cuba was a communist country. With rare exceptions it was illegal to run a business, own a car, or host a foreigner in your home. A French Canadian at the marina had been married to a Cuban woman for seven years yet he couldn't stay at her apartment because she didn't have a license to lodge foreigners! Nor could Cubans come aboard our boats. Still, the Cubans were wonderful. We enjoyed exploring the hotel zone and the adjoining town of Santa Marta. It was like a land that time forgot, with its pre-revolutionary cars, mostly 1950s Dodges, Chevys, Fords, and Chryslers, also some decrepit little Soviet-bloc cars and motorbikes. They kept them running because they weren't allowed to buy new ones. Many got around by horse and buggy. They played baseball a lot and rode around on bicycles.

After eight days at Varadero we felt ready to continue to Havana. The general rule was that navigators could only stop at marinas, but there weren't nearly enough to daysail from one to the next. Given our preference not to sail at night the *Guardafrontera* conceded us a *permiso especial* to anchor one night in a small harbor along the way provided we didn't go on land.

Our stopover was called Santa Cruz del Norte. We entered it at dusk, exhausted from a hard day's sail in scary winds. The opening was a narrow break in the tall, rocky shore. A *Guardafrontera* post guarded the right side of the entrance. The post's personnel stirred into action. "Go away, no tourism!" someone yelled. "We have permission!" I protested. After much shouting a soldier rowed out and took the paper. After his superiors had perused it we were informed that we should moor at their "dock," directly below the guard post. But it was a fallen-down jigsaw of jutting steel beams, a death trap for a boat of our configuration. After further disputation they said we could anchor immediately in front. Armed guards watched us all night.

At the first hint of light about twenty tiny wooden fishing boats with putt-putt motors started circling around us. They were chomping at the bit to go out and fish but the authorities, afraid they would escape to the U.S., required them to wait at the *Guardafrontera* station until daybreak. When red clouds streaked the eastern sky they all dispersed into the ocean, eager to lower their hand-lines.

We next stayed at a marina in a town called Tarará, ten miles before Havana. The opening was only a foot deep, impossible for most boats, so there weren't any other vessels. The plumbing and lighting fixtures didn't work but the people were friendly. Four or five guards watched over us every night. The surrounding community was mysterious! We were in the midst of a vast residential complex, nicely built and well tended, but the houses were empty. The single-family area was a Potemkin village, for show only. There were dormitories full of Chinese students learning Spanish, and a special area for Chernobyl victims. The twentieth anniversary of that nuclear disaster came up while we were there. A former president of the Ukraine presided over a memorial event. And that was it: Chinese students, disabled Chernobyl victims, guards, groundskeepers, and us. No regular Cubans were allowed!

We took an incredibly crowded bus into Havana. We walked for miles through this fascinating city, so full of ornate, dilapidated Spanish architecture. Vendors and shoppers thronged the dirt-floored markets. Pedestrians hung out along the wide waterfront sidewalk, where the ocean waves crashed and soaked us if we weren't quick to get out of the way.

We next sailed to Hemingway Marina, on the other side of Havana. This was Cuba's largest marina. We were one of perhaps a dozen inhabited boats from various countries. A delightful Argentine was on his way back home after buying a Morgan 44 in Florida. An elderly American who had married a fifteen-year-old Cuban girl drove us around looking for a small piece of aluminum plate on the black market. Boats were arriving from Mexico and leaving for Florida. We went out each day in search of places where we could use up our *moneda nacional* pesos. Now and then we found ice cream cones, pizza slices, sugar cane juice, or muffins, but usually they said, *"Acabó"* (all out). We ended up giving away $25 worth of those nearly worthless bills.

We were forbidden to go ashore at our next stop, a harbor used as a graveyard for dead ships. But at Cayo Levisa we were free to roam, so we stayed a week. It was a small island with tourist bungalows and a dock. We tied to a piling and did a lot of beachcombing. Finally the water was warm enough to swim!

Westward from Cayo Levisa the sea was shallow and sprinkled with mangrove islands, the *Archipielago de los Colorados*. The mountainous mainland was forbidden to us, but in this semi-protected gulf we traveled for five days unobserved. These patches of sand and tangled trees were too worthless and remote for the authorities to concern themselves with. The choice was often between staying closer in where the mangrove was tighter or further out where it was more open. The former was funner but the latter was faster. Both were very satisfying.

Pulling her through a tight spot in the Cuban mangrove

The archipelago terminated at Cabo San Antonio, Cuba's curling western cape. The only sign of man was a dock, some small neglected buildings, and a narrow road leading into a low, tropical forest. It was supposed to be a marina, but like that at Tarará it was empty. We walked along the road to a lighthouse at the very tip. To the south was the Caribbean Sea, our goal for so long. We still had nearly a month left on our sixty-day visas. We longed to sail the south coast of Cuba, which they say has unsurpassed diving, but our course lay west, across the Yucatán Channel.

Our second major crossing faced us: the Yucatán Passage. Mexico lay eighty miles west, further than we could travel in a day. Worse, a powerful current sets northward through that gap. Based on our experience crossing the Gulf Stream between Florida and the Bahamas, we decided to sail 120 miles southwest before turning west. This would double the distance but prevent us from being swept into the Gulf of Mexico.

Another yacht arrived during the evening. It was a middle-aged American named Jeff, a Colombian woman, and her ten-year-old son. Jeff confessed to being out of his depth in this sailing business; strong winds the past few days had demoralized them. He also alluded to a fear of drug traffickers. "They're using submarines now, you know that?" Nevertheless they were leaving for Mexico in the morning. Ginny and I hadn't intended to leave so soon; we weren't yet psyched for that crossing. But I suggested that we sail in tandem in order to provide mutual support. I explained our planned route. He seemed to agree.

At 6:00 a.m. I went aboard his boat. It was April 22, 2010. We listened to a forecast on his single sideband radio. It called for moderate east winds, quite suitable. Two hours later we got underway.

We cleared the cape together. Ginny and I then steered southwest per plan but Jeff continued northwest. We had VHF contact. "Jeff, we're heading southwest now, what's up?"

"The wind's pushing me north!"

"How can that be?" I asked. "The wind's easterly!"

He seemed evasive. Perhaps he didn't really want to accompany us. Then he said, "It's one of those Colombian submarines, they're right below us!"

"What? Describe what you're seeing!"

Except for some fragments he didn't come on anymore. Our plate was full; we could hardly linger out of curiosity. We never found out if he was avoiding us, crazy, or, less plausibly, under submarine attack.

It was hot and windy. All day we sailed with wind on the starboard quarter, a fast point of sail. When night came a half moon illuminated the waves, and stars facilitated steering. At one point I curled up on the bridge deck (the slightly crowned deck space between the cockpit and the cabin hatch) and napped. My inert body sagged this way and that with *Thurston's* gyrations, infusing my dreams with a sensation of turbulence and vulnerability. I sensed a large snake in the cockpit with me! It hissed in long, sustained exhalations. I woke. It was Ginny! Steering through those waves she was so nervous she was inhaling and exhaling through clenched teeth, like a hissing snake! We were giddy with terror and exhilaration.

Morning found us at the end of our southwest leg. So far we had stayed in waters two to three miles deep. Now it was time to cut west across the relative shallows. Due to our detour the north-setting Gulf Stream would favor us. The wind built to 20-25 knots, the waves to eight feet. We reduced sail by more than half and still did six knots! We sliced diagonally down the wave fronts, careful not to broach. We bailed, sometimes scooping up little fish that had washed aboard. A little land bird hovered fitfully overhead, but was too afraid of us to land. Would we arrive before a second night overtook us?

Finally the mammoth hotels of Cancún began popping up over the horizon. As the sun set we rounded a point and anchored in calm water. Lovely inns soared above us, blocking the wind. Clients splashed about. The sound of dinners and cocktails wafted over the water. We stripped off the soggy clothes we'd been wearing for thirty-six hours. Ginny hadn't slept the whole time. My butt had sores where my ilia bones stuck out. We lay down in the cabin and relished the peacefulness. Mexico! It had taken us two years to get back. From here the coral reef extends south almost to Guatemala!

In the morning we cleared customs at Isla Mujeres, a slender island three miles long. The officials took all our food away except our powdered milk, claiming import restrictions. But the local stores offered solace. After Cuba they seemed to burst with fruits, juices, and cookies! Internet was everywhere. The people were Mayan, short and beaming like brown-skinned cherubs, relatively affluent due to their jobs in the tourism industry. The main road running the length of the island buzzed with locals on scooters wearing colorful plastic helmets, and with sunburned North Americans in beach attire driving golf carts. There were twenty or so cruising sailboats in the harbor, but the hurricane season was approaching so one by one they left for Texas, Florida, or the Rio Dulce. We had finally escaped winter! Only the constant wind and our awning made the heat bearable. We wore full-coverage, light-colored cotton clothes and Keens beach shoes. We learned where to buy supplies and get things made out of metal. Saltwater had shorted out our flexible solar panel so we replaced it with a rigid one. To ease steering we had a "tiller-tamer" fabricated. It consisted of an aluminum "comb" attached to the top of the lazarette (via a hinge so it could be folded down when not in use) and a small blade attached to the underside of the tiller. To set the tiller-tamer we tilted the comb up, held the tiller at the desired angle, and lowered it so the blade engaged the appropriate slot in the comb.

We also laid plans to get married in Belize, it having become obvious that we were permanently in love. For two years we'd been living as intimately as two people can live and had discovered only more and more good things. The voyage was our joint creation. Family and friends would be coming down for the wedding.

On May 14 we headed south along the Mayan Riviera. Stretching a hundred miles from Cancún to Tulum, this stretch of Caribbean coastline is popular with tourists. Sometimes we sailed behind the coral reef, sometimes in front of it. We slept in sandy coves that hadn't been discovered yet and snorkeled along shorelines of low limestone rock. Mangrove often fringed the shore, their roots dipping into the water like sharp, slimy fingers.

Tulum is a beautiful Mayan site, with ruins on a cliff overlooking the sea. The central tower was a lighthouse marking an entrance through the reef. We had stayed in Tulum in 2008 when we toured the Yucatán by truck and canoe. This time we tried sleeping aboard but it was too rough, so we anchored just outside the surf in water up to our waists and pitched our tent on a wooded sand dune. A young Mexican couple with dreadlocks stayed in a neighboring tent. They were carefree street musicians, perfecting their act. I got out my accordion and played tunes with them.

The lighthouse at Tulum marks a pass through the reef.

It was less populated south of Tulum. At a river mouth we took down our masts and rowed under a bridge. Inside we followed a series of lagoons that paralleled the coast. Their shallowness made windward sailing difficult because we couldn't sufficiently immerse our leeboards or rudder blade, but we could always row. Finally a narrow, winding passage led to Bahía de la Ascension, a vast bay with reefs and islands at its mouth.

To reach the next big bay we had to sail the open sea again. This was our roughest day to date. To explain how we coped with the splash I have to describe *Thurston's* cockpit drain. It was above the waterline while she was stationary, so at rest the cockpit was self-draining. Underway, however, *Thurston* squatted, putting the drain a couple inches below the waterline. If the splash was minor we kept the plug in and bailed as necessary, but when the bailing became constant we removed the plug and accepted the water sloshing around our ankles, knowing it wouldn't get any worse. That's what we did as we bashed our way from Bahía de la Ascension to Bahía del Espíritu Santo.

Our anchorage in the latter bay was typical of many along this lee shore. The wind and waves came straight onto the land. The reef broke up the waves, but much energy filtered through. The lagoon behind was four feet deep. The distance to the beach was sufficient for new waves to form from the constant wind, but the lagoon continued to shoal. The last hundred yards were less than eighteen inches deep with a bed of eel grass. The shallow bottom kept toppling the waves until no energy was left where we anchored in a foot of water. Ah, the blessings of shoal draft! We walked for miles along the uninhabited beach, opening coconuts for their water.

Traveling inside the reef was calmer and we could stop whenever we wanted. Unfortunately the lagoon is scattered with coral heads just below the surface. We kept a constant lookout, often swerving at the last second. *Thurston's* bottom got plenty of new gashes. At Mahahual, southerly outpost of the touristy Costa Maya, a new cruise ship pier had been completed but no ship was in just then. The hucksters in the restaurants and artisan shops along the seafront walkway focused all their spiels on us. Snorkeling we saw turtles, nurse sharks, barracuda, and countless colorful little reef fish each standing sentinel over its own little niche in the coral. The clear water revealed a bottom sloping steeply into open ocean.

Speaking of great snorkeling, in a way we were there due to my bad lower back. In 2007 my doctors had called it "degenerative disc disease." One of them showed me an X-ray. "See this dislocation between your fourth and fifth lumbars?" he asked. "I wish I could wrap that joint with an iron band of muscle. Swimming might do it." A major goal of our 2007-08 truck trip through Mexico and Belize was to accomplish that. We carried a canoe on the roof and followed the coastlines. I swam an hour in the morning and an hour in the evening; Ginny swam nearly as much. My body changed drastically. My gut and butt shrank and my torso developed a sheath of muscle. We constantly sought new spots to swim, but most of the coast lacked public access. Nor could the canoe take us to the offshore reefs. So we returned to the States and acquired *Thurston*. In the interim our bodies had reverted to relative flabbiness. Resuming our old swimming regimen felt great, but wasn't really necessary for my back anymore. Swimming or not, I'd learned how to live with my squished discs, and they weren't getting any worse. Back therapy didn't explain our presence there anymore. The snorkeling had become a goal, not a means. The voyage itself was taking over, and swimming would remain one of the reasons we cruised.

We now fulfilled a long-held dream. The map showed an atoll called Chinchorro Bank eighteen miles to windward. It was seven miles wide and twenty-three miles long! They say it and similar formations in Belize are the only atolls in the Western Hemisphere. What does such a place look like? How crystalline was the water? We decided to find out. Knowing it may be off-limits we didn't inquire about permits. The bank lay east, and the Sea Pearl doesn't point well into the wind. Also, a branch of the Gulf Stream flows north at two knots through the strait between Mahahual and Banco Chinchorro.

We got underway early. The GPS showed we made 2.5 knots during our port tacks (wind coming from port), against the current, and 4.5 knots on our starboard tacks, with the current. All day we bashed. It was too hot for foul weather gear, too sunny for bare skin. We wore cotton clothes and got rashes. After nine hours the water finally changed from deep blue to shallow green. It was dark when we anchored in the lee of Cayo Centro, an island in the middle of the bank.

We found ourselves in a vast marine wilderness. We swam along the mangrove shore and explored an unoccupied fishing village on stilts, never touching land. Next we sailed out to the eastern edge of the atoll and tried the swimming there. It was too dangerous; the waves beat too heavily on the jagged coral and an east-setting current kept threatening to push me over the edge into the deep Atlantic where I might not find a way back. So we turned to the hundreds of coral patches scattered over the interior of the bank. Each was an almost-island rising from a depth of about twenty feet. We sighted all the familiar reef fishes plus some new ones. No one bothered us until the fourth day, when a *Comision Nacional de Areas Naturales* boat approached. An official said, "You are in a biosphere reserve! Please leave, and no more swimming!" We complied except that as we sailed back over the western drop-off we couldn't resist jumping in one last time. This edge was calm and scenic. The floor dropped from ten feet rapidly into great depths. Coral rocks with a high coverage of live coral studded the sandy flanks. Visibility was seventy feet!

We followed the mainland to Xcalak, a village near Belize. On June 16, 2010, we got our clearance concluding eight lovely weeks in Mexico. The border with Belize was nearby. The border starts at the sea and follows a meandering mangrove channel called Boca Bacalar Chico. We were familiar with it from when we canoed the area. To take advantage of interior waterways we wiggled westward into it. Glad to be back, Ginny kissed the first Belizean mangrove we accidentally collided with! We got lost in a dead end too narrow to deploy our oars, and had to paddle and pole back against a current until we got back on track. Finally we reached Chetumal Bay and sailed to the tourist town of San Pedro on Ambergris Caye.

We were waiting at Immigration the following morning when the officer arrived. "Oh mon you guys, it's so early," he said. He rubbed the sleep out of his eyes, decided against searching our boat because he didn't want to get wet, and issued us visas. San Pedro's narrow dirt streets were starting to fill. Soon tourists were riding around in golf carts holding drinks while locals of Mexican origin drove around with big flags and noisemakers to celebrate a soccer victory in their native country. We sailed thirty miles northwest to Corozal to visit some friends and perform a legal marriage in a small courtroom. Then we returned to the cayes (pronounced "keys"). We got to Caye Caulker four days in advance of our ritual, as opposed to legal, wedding, and tied up to a shallow shore at the south end of the island.

Friends and family started arriving from Seattle, St. Louis, and Los Angeles. In twos and threes they flew to Belize City then took a "water taxi" to Caye Caulker. Four small houses had been reserved for them. We had delicious dinners together but split into groups for day outings. Some explored Mayan ruins, others went snorkeling or sailing.

On July 1 we had the wedding in the garden by the main house. Ginny's mom emceed skits on the themes of Exploration, Euphoria, Insanity, and Love. My dad played the accordion. My cousin Kristy sang. Ginny's sister Carley, an ordained minister via the internet, tied the knot. There was juggling and hacky-sacking. We were few but talented. I'd felt guilty about obliging them all to travel to Belize for our wedding, but they seemed to appreciate the excursion.

Friends Lena and Jesse juggle at our wedding in Caye Caulker

After a week they started trickling away. We accompanied each group to the dock to see them off until it was just us again. For our honeymoon we stayed another two weeks working on the boat while living aboard. Among other improvements we made a mount for our handheld GPS and painted the cabin top white, the best color for the tropics. Then we provisioned for a trip to Turneffe and Lighthouse reefs, atolls like Chinchorro Bank.

A hard day of beating to windward took us beyond the horizon to Turneffe Reef, a thirty-mile-long galaxy of mangrove islands encased in an oval-shaped barrier reef. We sailed up the west side swimming in the clear water and anchoring in protected spots. Among the many crazy things we saw were small fishes with clear bodies and yellow heads that emerge from holes in the sand and go back in tail first! When a storm hit we holed up for two days on the northernmost caye. There was a lighthouse there but no one was around.

Next we sailed twenty miles further east to Lighthouse Reef. We anchored off an island at the south end and swam along the vertical wall that hems the reef there. It went straight down for hundreds of feet! Then we sailed up to the Great Blue Hole, a *cenote* (collapsed limestone cave) in the middle of the reef. Unlike *cenotes* on land the surrounding area is five to ten feet underwater. In order to avoid having to hire a guide we waited at a distance until late afternoon. When all the other boats left we rowed to the Hole and tied to a buoy. The chasm was a quarter mile in diameter, perfectly round, deep blue. Without oxygen tanks we couldn't plumb its stalagmite-festooned depths, but we swam the drop-off, diving down to where the vertical wall curves inward to form an overhang. They say the flooded cavern is over 400 feet deep!

We often saw lobster divers. They sailed brightly-painted, gaff-rigged, wooden sloops built in the village of Sarteneja, near Corozal. A Sarteneja boat carried ten or so young, brown-skinned, Spanish-speaking divers. Each diver paddled a small dugout. They looked under rocks, tying their canoes' bow lines around their waists while diving. We enjoyed their company in the anchorages we shared. They dove for a living, we for fun.

The eastern barrier reef is shallow, with coral heads right at the surface. Here we swam in the cuts and the deep water just outside. The corals on the western barrier are deeper and the bottom drops off more steeply. I loved the west-side wall dives! The interior was shallow with hundreds of patch reefs. They grow to within inches of the surface, making them hazardous even in shallow-draft *Thurston*. Once we accidentally sailed onto one. We had to stand on coral heads to pull her off, an ecological no-no because the coral is fragile. Thereafter we navigated such areas only with a high sun and a clear sky, in which light the shallow coral rocks are a chocolate brown surrounded by turquoise.

On August 10 we returned to Turneffe Reef. Someone had recommended Caye Bokel, the southernmost island in that group. There we pulled up to a dock in front of a low shack. Its windows were large with top-hinged plywood shutters. An elderly man came out. Like most Belizeans he was of mostly African descent and spoke both English and an English-based Creole. "Are you hungry?" he asked. He fed me lobsters he'd caught in his traps and fried plantains for Ginny. He'd lived there alone for years and appreciated our company. "Nice to have someone to cook for," he said.

Our next port of call was Belize City, on the mainland. The harbor is built around Haulover Creek, a secondary mouth of the Belize River. Just downstream of the Swing Bridge (so named for its manner of opening) a hundred or so poles had been driven into the river bottom. Sarteneja boats were tied bow and stern at these poles. We tied likewise and pumped up the dinghy.

Thus began four days in that much-maligned metropolis of seventy thousand souls, by far Belize's largest city. It looked Old-World. The narrow streets were laced with concrete drainage channels. The buildings were faintly Victorian yet grotesquely dilapidated. We were moored in its most bustling quarter. Seamen congregated by the Swing Bridge. Beggars hit on us. Creole fellows fell in alongside and exuberantly declared their brotherhood toward us. We were friendly yet firm. We didn't want guides or drugs or people to watch our boat. We just wanted to complete our chores.

We looked up a fellow sailor named Kirk, a Texan whom we'd socialized with in Mexico and Caye Caulker. Among other oddities he believed the CIA was constantly after him. He was garrulous, a rich kid who had never grown up, a generous kook. His sailboat and ours seemed to be the only cruisers left on that coast now that it was hurricane season. Unfortunately he'd run aground outside the city. It took him two weeks and the assistance of a tugboat to get off. Meanwhile the authorities charged him for not reporting the incident and for a visa infraction. Now he was staying at the Radisson Hotel, pacing back and forth in mental anguish. He ended up paying huge fines and legal fees and almost went to jail. We would see him again.

Our last day at the Swing Bridge was marred by young hoodlums, probably the same kids who had been sneaking aboard and pawing through our stuff while we were gone. On this occasion we were relaxing in the cockpit when they started pelting us with fish guts from the back end of a restaurant on shore. Then they moved over to the bridge and started pelting rocks. We ducked inside the cabin until they drifted off. How humiliating, to cower before a pack of ten-year-old boys!

Haulover Creek viewed from Swing Bridge.
Thurston is in foreground. The others are lobster boats.

Belize's coast runs north and south. Immediately offshore is a shallow channel five to ten miles wide. Next comes a band of small, flat islands. Many are only mangrove trees immersed in water. The islands terminate at the barrier reef, which is a band of dead and living coral awash with ocean swells. It is possible to exit the reef only at the passes, which are the supreme dive spots because of the rich sea life and dramatic underwater topography. We continued south through the islands, carrying enough food and water for two weeks at a time. The fruits and vegetables gave out much sooner, of course, forcing us onto less appetizing meals toward the end of each leg.

We returned to the mainland at Dangriga, alias Stann Creek. This place was relaxed and funky, but had some absurdly aggressive

SOUTH . . .

panhandlers. One day an elderly Creole gentleman followed us around trying to give me an opened coconut to drink. "My brother, coconut for you!" he cried. "No thanks," I kept saying. When we went into the library he followed us and continued his entreaties, now sticking it under my nose. "Take it!" he urged. It did smell good! Against my better judgment I took a sip. It was cool and faintly sweet. "I'm sorry, no food or drink in the library," said the librarian. Bracing myself for the confrontation over price I went out to the porch, drained the coconut, and offered the man fifty cents. "Two dollah! Two dollah!" he screeched, no longer fraternal. He remained outside the library ranting at us for some time while we did our research, trying to ignore his ruckus.

Exiting Stann Creek was tough. There was a strong onshore wind and the mouth was too narrow to tack. We kept the masts down to lessen wind resistance and rowed over the bar. The boat kept wanting to turn sideways to the wind. We anchored to keep from being blown back while raising the masts. A wave broke over the boat, filling the cockpit. I stood with my legs wide apart on the foredeck. Ginny got low and gripped my belt from behind, giving me fore-aft stability. I hoisted the mast vertical in a series of upward shifts and dropped it into its socket. We repeated with the mizzen. Then we beat out to the chain of islands.

Belize's southern waters are deeper, often sixty feet, but contain numerous steep-sided underwater hills. Their flat tops are slightly below sea level, good for diving on. Corals surrounded the low islands. The wind died, as it often does in late summer. We took turns rowing in the excruciating heat with the tarp up to block the sun. For weeks the temperature was in the nineties by day and in the eighties by night. I got heat rash, maddeningly itchy patches on my arms and torso. We restocked again at Placencia, then sailed back out to the barrier reef and south along it, to Ranguana Caye and the Sapodilla Cayes, a widely dispersed group. These were real islands with sand and coconut trees, not just swamp! Here ended the coral reef we'd been following since Cancún.

How to anchor at night was a quandary. We needed shelter because *Thurston* rocked uncomfortably in waves. We passed many nights rolling around like rag-dolls in our three-foot by eight-foot bed, Ginny with her head forward, I with mine aft, our legs overlapping. The islands, often no larger than a football field, could protect us from one direction, but the wind usually changed direction during the night. Violent lightning storms were common. The bugs also complicated anchoring. We wanted to sleep with the bow nudged onto the beach to get the most protection from the island, but that put us among the mosquitoes. Even a hundred yards offshore they found us. We could retreat into the cabin, which had a mosquito net, but it was too hot inside. Our worse night was on Carey Caye, where we anchored on a seemingly bug-free shore. Then a storm hit. When the thunder and rain stopped a plague of no-see-ums erupted. They were small enough to crawl through the mosquito net, so we had to keep mosquito coils burning. Between the rocking, heat rashes, and insects we rarely slept well.

Our ninety days worth of visa were nearly over. Our final stop was Punta Gorda, at the terminus of the road that runs north and south through Belize. The Mayans in the surrounding villages grew cocoa beans and stored them in a warehouse in town. They gave us a handful of the dry, germinated beans. They were the size of a thumb, with the texture of dates and the taste of raw chocolate. "Who do you sell them to?" we asked. "Cadbury's," we were told.

The Mayans were capable of mayhem. At a Catholic revival meeting in the town square the speaker talked about *"los niños perdidos"* ("the lost children"). We found the story in the local paper. Five days before a brother and sister, both under ten, had been sent to town to sell limes. They were never seen again. A woman claiming to have soothsaying powers accused an American couple running a center for the rescue of endangered crocodiles a few miles from town. She divined that they had fed the children to their crocodiles! A bus-load of angry villagers descended upon the croc farm. No one was around, but they found limes! Considering this sufficient proof they burned the place down and killed the reptiles. The soothsayer was subsequently arrested for "pretending to be a fortune-teller!"

Tall, green mountains now showed themselves to the southwest. At their foot, seventeen miles away across the Bahía Amatrique, was our next town: Livingston, Guatemala.

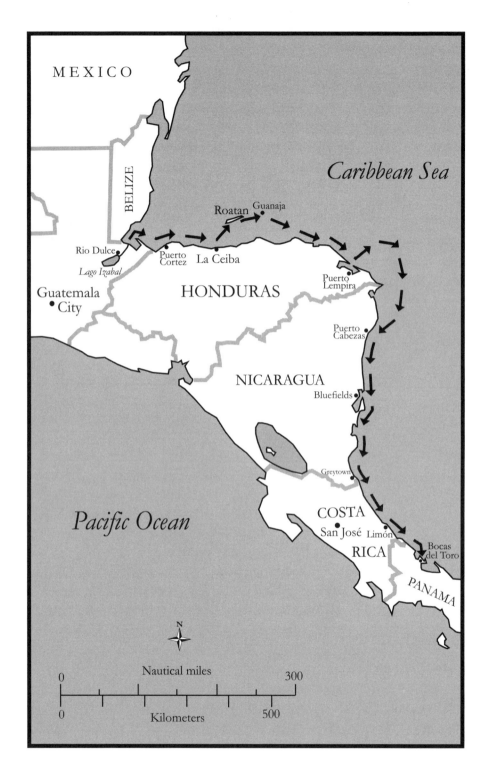

Chapter 3
. . . AND PANAMA, STILL NO MOTOR

It was September 9, 2010. The snorkeling had been great but we had come to the end of the reefs and didn't feel like stopping. We would always relish opportunities to swim, but the voyage itself now absorbed us. We had a great boat and knew the wonderful things you can do with such a tool. So, accepting the first of several large mission creeps that would ensue in the coming years, we continued south. The winds would be mostly favorable until we reached Panama, at the southwest corner of the Caribbean. We would have to make another decision then.

The sun glared on a flat sea as we took turns rowing. The mountains of Guatemala turned from blue to green as they loomed up. Rounding a headland we entered the bay at the mouth of the Rio Dulce. To our right was Livingston.

The waterfront was a jumble of docks and buildings. We tied to iron bars jutting out from an abandoned factory. The town was steep. Some of the people were Spanish-speaking mestizos, others were Mayans, but the biggest share seemed to be Garifunas, a black Caribbean people with their own language. After getting ninety-day visas we sat in an open restaurant and had scrambled eggs, beans, rice, and sweet plantain for only twenty *quetzales* ($2.50 U.S.). Women washed their clothes in a specially designed municipal facility. It consisted of an ankle-deep pool with a roof over it and a double row of concrete scrubbing surfaces. The cool water, shade, and socializing clearly lightened their labor.

We were curious to see the Rio Dulce, a famous hurricane hole among cruisers. It is a short river. For two days we sailed and rowed against the current. The river flowed through a winding canyon with sheer, forested walls. We passed boys in dugout canoes tugging hand lines. We reached a small lake surrounded by low jungle, then Lago Izabal, which is twenty miles long and ten miles wide. A tall bridge crosses the river where it issues from the lake. The town of Rio Dulce is on the right, or northwest, side of the bridge.

The town was small and crowded. It had one long, narrow street packed with stores, cattle trucks, and motorbikes. Mayan women in traditional garb sold food on the street. Drivers and pedestrians slowly squeezed through the crowd. Dust, diesel fumes, and the smell of cooking chicken assailed our nostrils. At the north end of town the highway continued through vast forests to Flores and the ruins of Tikal. South it led to the more populous Guatemalan highlands.

North American and European yachts moored at marinas along the river. Some owners lived aboard, others left their boats in storage. We tied up at a public dock under the bridge until someone stole our anchor, chain, and two hundred feet of nylon braid in broad daylight. Thereafter we stayed at a marina on the southeast side of the bridge. There was no dry land in the vicinity, just forested swamp. The docks and over-water structures were made from rough planks. A dozen or so live-aboards and a few Guatemalan workers lived there. I set up a mosquito net over a chair in the common area. Here I often read after dinner, alone in the near-darkness or with one or two other guests.

The other sailors got to town via their dinghies. Ginny and I got there by wading through the swamp. One route involved walking on rotten planks precariously elevated over the water. A sign along the way said (translating) "Five dollars passage." We got through once without that intervening owner hassling us for the money, but thereafter we went a different way that required hitching up our pants to our thighs. Either way, upon emerging from the swamp we crossed a field, cut through a school yard, and walked across a half-mile-long bridge into town. It was noisy there compared to our semi-deserted marina.

We found a new anchor and related gear. We varnished and painted, adding green enamel accents to *Thurston's* color scheme. The rowing seat broke, so we made a new one. The mosquito net that covers the cabin door tore so we made one of those too. We'd lived aboard for ten months, and our boat work had shifted from debugging to on-going maintenance.

I decided to ship my accordion home and buy a guitar. The squeeze-box was too hard to get in and out of its storage place near the bow and there was no comfortable position in which to play it aboard. A guitar would be more practical, so we took a bus to Guatemala City. The six-hour ride cost only $7.50 each. We stayed at a $14-a-night hotel in the historic district. We walked and bussed all over the city locating shipping agencies and music stores. I sent the accordion home and bought a small guitar, what they call a *requinto,* having resolved to learn that instrument. Much lighter and more portable, it would be my companion for the next four years. We also got new binoculars, T-shirts, and shoes. In Guatemala City's cool climate my rashes went away! I'd never known what they were, but their disappearance now indicated heat rash. Fortunately I was never much plagued by them again.

There was fine old architecture around the Plaza Mayor, which is like a smaller version of Mexico City's Socalo. Vendors crowded the many market districts. We discovered a vast auto repair district, a jewelry district, and even a bridal district with storefront after storefront of mannequins displaying nuptial gowns. We treated ourselves to cinema outings and drank beer at a Chinese restaurant that doubled as a working-class sports bar. In our week there we got to know the city pretty well.

Back at Rio Dulce we cruised Lago Izabal for ten days. There was little wind, so we rowed west along the north shore of the lake to the town of El Estor. Forested mountains ringed the lake, yet the banks were low. We camped in coves and creeks, and explored the mouths of the Rio Polochic, where monkeys howled in the tall trees. We visited a Mayan village where the people lived in plank-and-thatch houses. Everyone was at the soccer field, where a match was underway. The players wore team uniforms. The women wore full, shoulder-strap blouses and long skirts of intricate hand-weave. The toddlers wore nothing at all.

Guatemala's Caribbean coast is short. We cleared out at Livingston then continued to Honduras. Its coast runs four hundred miles due east into the prevailing trade winds with few harbors. It would be difficult to reach refuges before nightfall. We had considered buying a small outboard motor but the extra weight and clutter deterred us, so we continued under oars and sails.

The first night we easily entered a small river mouth. The second night was more difficult. At the Rio Motagua, which forms the border with Honduras, we angled seaward to round the sand bars at its mouth, then entered a channel just deep enough for the swells to roll in without toppling over. Halfway in we jumped into the waist-deep water and pulled her through, resisting the waves which knocked us about and threatened to tear *Thurston* from our grasp.

Inside the water was calm. The land was flat, the river wide and shallow. The only sign of man was a thatched lean-to and a motor launch in the distance. Honduras had a bad reputation. We ducked into a small side channel near the mouth, hoping no one had seen us. After a couple hundred yards it dead-ended in swamp. We took the masts down, mopped up, and unwound as it got dark.

We heard a motor. "Damn, someone's following us in! Would you get me the machete, babe?" I said. She set it down by me. I sat in the stern facing the intruders. I got out our powerful flashlight and shined it in their eyes as they came up, motoring slowing through the tall grass. *"Que cosa?"* (What's up?) I yelled. There was no escape. It would be impossible to swim, walk, or boat away. A launch with three men and a boy bumped into us. They gripped our gunwale, their lean, brown faces a couple feet from mine. They were silent and expressionless except for one who babbled nervously. He said that they'd come to see if we needed any help, but it sounded like an afterthought. I said we were sleeping there and left my machete in plain sight. After a parting pleasantry they backed away.

The tension lingered, but the evening was beautiful. A breeze rustled the reeds. Crabs, crickets, and cockroaches climbed aboard from the surrounding vegetation, requiring many minor evictions. Something larger swam by, bumping into the hull. We couldn't see it. Nearby was a tree in which many white storks were roosting. It was November 4, 2010.

The next day, as we cut across a large bight toward Puerto Cortez, the wind built up to thirty-seven knots. We had never experienced nearly so much wind. We rolled up our sails until only tiny triangles remained, and still shot through the bounding waves at over six knots.

Puerto Cortez was open to this terrible west wind. The lee was a rocky shore. We anchored just shy of it and pondered what to do. Scanning with our binoculars we glimpsed an inlet at the bottom of the bay which, in our anchored orientation, lay to port. "We should be able to enter that," I said. Unfortunately, the wind was blowing too hard to pull the boat up to the anchor. *Thurston* bucked as waves broke over the bow. To better combine our strengths I tried to row while Ginny pulled at the line. *Thurston* inched painfully forward, pitching and yawing. Our muscles ached. When the line was nearly vertical Ginny cleated off. Whenever the bow dropped into a trough we took in slack. The anchor had buried itself deeply, probably into firm sand, but after ten minutes with the bow jerking up every few seconds it broke out. Ready to go, we carefully fell onto the starboard tack. (If we'd been caught on the port tack we would have had to quickly tack or jibe, neither of which would have been safe in that situation.) We zoomed to the bottom of the bay and turned right into the tidal creek. We were relieved but also consternated, for we found ourselves in the middle of a naval base! Fortunately, the brass allowed us to stay there for two days while we waited for the storm to blow over.

Now cleared into Honduras, our next refuge was Laguna Diamante, in a remote national park thirty miles east. The coast was generally low but here a sharp spur of mountain jutted into the ocean. Midway along this razorback ridge was a fifty-yard-wide gap with seas breaking heavily on both sides. Shooting through, we found ourselves in a large lagoon. One side was bounded by the ridge we had passed through, the rest was surrounded by flat mangrove. There were no boats or houses, only an empty thatched hut. The place felt sinister, so we left in the morning. Our hunch was prescient. A couple weeks later a Canadian yachtsman was murdered there by four men in a motorboat. His daughter, the only other person aboard, survived. Laguna Diamante was a beautiful trap.

The next town, Tela, had no harbor. It was too rough to sleep, so we anchored outside the surf and swam in with a waterproof duffle bag containing clothes and necessities. We walked the streets in dripping swimsuits until we found a cheap hotel. At an internet place we studied again this coast's many stream mouths via Google Earth. Which we might safely enter would depend on the strength and direction of the wind on the day in question, but at least we would know where to look.

There would be no sure thing until La Ceiba, forty-five miles away. Too far. The western-most of the Bay Islands, Utila, was closer so we headed there. First there was no wind, then too much. Night closed in with heavy rain. We sailed blind, watching the compass with a headlamp, scrutinizing the GPS, shivering. Finally, lights! At 10:00 p.m. we entered the harbor and anchored within wading distance of land.

Utila is famous for its coral reef and unique social blend. Like Belize the islands were settled by Brits, and English is still spoken. Spanish- and Garifuna-speaking Hondurans came later to work in the tourism and fishing industries. The town consisted of one long, crescent-shaped street lined with dive shops and restaurants. We rested there for five days, snorkeling and hiking.

Several problems with *Thurston* had surfaced. We heard there was a good shipyard in La Ceiba, the largest city on the coast, so we went there. The mainland was a narrow plain backed by steep, lush mountains. We entered through a pair of jetties and continued past docks thronged with rusty fishing boats. Mangrove creeks radiated into the upland. The La Ceiba Shipyard occupied a peninsula between two such creeks. A Travelift moved *Thurston* onto land.

La Ceiba, population 130,000, was once the center of operations for the Standard Fruit Company. We often took a bus downtown. The streets were busy, the market crowded. Many utility vaults and manholes were missing their covers, obliging us to watch our step. There were too many taxis for the number of patrons; they constantly honked at us as they passed. We acquainted ourselves with the local businesses, and settled on a favorite restaurant. The typical meal was meat, rice, beans, and fried plantains. In the center of town was a small park featuring the busts of various Honduran heroes. The earth was beaten bare except in the corners less trampled, where coarse crabgrass subsisted.

On the shipyard's flat gravel surface lay about thirty commercial and recreational boats. Some were being repaired, others were in storage or abandoned. Welding torches were forever sparking and crackling.

Thurston (so small she is barely visible) getting hauled out in La Ceiba

Camp Drip, La Ceiba Shipyard, Honduras

Much bottom paint was applied with long-handled rollers, for the boats were quite tall up on their blocks. American and European crews came and went. As usual, we'd thought our last stint of boat work had earned us a long period of uninterrupted cruising, but problems had surfaced all too soon, and as long as we were hauled out with boat-building materials available we might as well lengthen our To Do list. *Thurston's* bottom had gel coat blisters and gashes, so we grinded, fiberglassed, and painted. We had stiffening brackets and a new Sumbrella awning fabricated. We got new foam for our cabin cushions and replaced our tent zippers. We bought new equipment over the internet and had it forwarded to us by Ginny's mom in Los Angeles. Thus we obtained an inflatable kayak (less bulky than the dinghy given to us in Marathon), a single-sideband radio receiver for weather forecasts, and charts of the coast down to Colombia. Lois also included little gifts and decorations to enliven our holidays. We would spend Thanksgiving and Christmas in La Ceiba.

We called it Camp Drip. To get out of the rain we placed *Thurston* under a huge catamaran. *Thurston,* our tent, and some makeshift tables and blocks for seating easily fit under the deck between its twin hulls, but the deck was perforated with little holes. We set out buckets to catch the drips. The roof dripped even when it wasn't raining because the catamaran had filled with rainwater which constantly dribbled out. We were living under a leaky swimming pool! We learned where to duck so as not to hit our heads, and where to step to avoid puddles.

On January 6, 2011, our work finally done, we sailed the thirty miles to Roatan, largest of the Bay Islands. Its southwest tip was green and hilly, closely encircled by a coral reef. We found a pass leading to a small cove with perfect wave protection. I donned mask and flippers. The pass sloped down through the nearly vertical coral wall into clear blue depths! The fish and corals were similar to those in Belize.

In the coming days we explored Coxen Hole and French Harbor, the larger towns. They boasted good sidewalks and no litter! The people spoke English and Spanish equally. As we continued along Roatan's forty-mile length the wind was on our nose. Curious as to just how close to the wind we were able to sail, we analyzed our zigzag track as recorded in our GPS. Our average angle to the wind was a terrible sixty degrees *made good,* that is, with slippage and adverse current incorporated. For the present it didn't matter because we could stop in any of a number of coves, but later *Thurston's* poor windward performance would exact a toll.

On January 15 we sailed across the ten-mile gap to the next island, Guanaja. Two divergent swell patterns were running. Whenever the crests of the two patterns coincided we shot up on a surprisingly tall wave, and whenever the troughs coincided we dropped into a hole. Suddenly a fierce southwester sprang up. Donning our safety harnesses, we rotated the main mast eight times and the mizzen mast five times, reducing sail area by two thirds. Still we flew over that grotesquely uneven plain the color of pewter and steel wool.

Guanaja was mountainous and heavily wooded. We passed The Caye, where most of the people live, and continued another mile to a bay where a half-dozen sailboats lay at anchor. We had heard much about Guanaja and looked forward to seeing familiar faces. Sure enough, as we sailed past a tall, stately restaurant at the foot of the bight a cheer went up!

Stopping, we were greeted by cruising friends we had made in Isla Mujeres and La Ceiba, and by managers Claus and Annette. The latter were a fun-loving couple who had moved there fifteen years before. They invited us to stay in their dinghy basin and use the adjoining barbecue shelter and water faucet. They and Hans Pico, who owned an adjoining farm and pizza bar, were from Baden-Wurttemberg, Germany. Hans, who knew the Mosquito Coast, advised us to follow certain interconnecting canals there, and to have the Indians make us bows and arrows from their local woods. He felt we would be in more danger once we left Guanaja. "The only tourists here are we sailors so the locals treat us great" said Gar, an Alaskan with a ring in his ear and a bandanna wrapped tightly around his head. He had anchored there eleven years before and never left. At one time or another all the old-timers unburdened themselves to us regarding Hurricane Mitch. In 1998 it plastered the island with 180-knot winds for two days, killing the forests and ruining the houses. Afterward everyone worked together to rebuild, forming deep bonds. The sunsets from Claus and Annette's bar were exquisite, with a light screen of tropical landscaping in the foreground, the island's lush hills to the right, and The Caye in the middle, beside the sun.

The Caye, a sort of Third World Venice, lay a quarter mile from the main island. We tied up in a bedlam of broken boats and collapsed piers. There were no streets, only a maze of radial walkways accessing the dilapidated two-story homes that occupied every square foot. The walkways turned and tapered as they neared the island's edge, each turn revealing another entry, until terminating at some final weather-stained house on stilts. A network of narrow canals provided drainage and canoe parking. Private scenes presented themselves in doorways and in tiny courts, but the people didn't seem to mind us. It was Thursday, the day the weekly supply ship came. The public dock was piled with goods. Young men carted boxes, and shoppers lugged their purchases home.

We summed up our financial records. Traveling aboard *Thurston* throughout 2010 had cost us $17,000, under $50 per day. Much of that we had spent improving our boat. To confirm her sea-worthiness we now tipped her over intentionally, fully loaded, in the small-boat basin. She refused to turn turtle and was easily righted, especially if I removed the masts.

Capsize test, Guanaja, Honduras

We also went on hikes and picnicked with new friends. There was a big birthday party for Annette. An instrumental group consisting of Claus and some friends played American rock classics well into the night. We sat at the bar drinking dark hefeweisen and listened to impassioned stories from Hans Pico, a former professional motorcycle racer, now a farmer and restaurateur. He had long tangles of straw-colored hair and a booming voice that belied his nurturing spirit, for he tended horses, cattle, parrots, pigeons, chickens, ducks, and dogs. His eighteen-year-old son, Hannes, baked the island's best pizzas in an outdoor, wood-fired oven.

We loved Guanaja best of all the places we'd been so far. The people were almost painfully lovable, painfully because we knew that we would soon move on, and that forever after we would regret not getting to know them better, not having spent more of our lives with them. This parting was delayed while the wind remained from the ESE, which was no good for us. But when north and northeast winds were forecast we planned our departure. By leaving at midnight we hoped to reach the mouth of the Rio Sico the following day. At the last minute Annette, still up, brought us a loaf of homemade bread and a bottle of wine. Hans and Hannes came over with a basket of oranges and dried mangoes. We sucked up our guts, brushed off our tears, and climbed aboard.

The distance was sixty-five miles, the course ESE. As we rowed away the harbor was calm, but further out the wind swirled around the mountainous island to reach us. Stars shone here and there through cloud gaps. The sea built, squalls hit. We reefed once, twice, a third time. Ginny curled up on deck, cold, wet, nauseous. She couldn't keep her eyes open, but she couldn't sleep either. It was much rougher than we had anticipated. We passed a horrid night.

In the morning the wind veered and died. Cloud banks concealed the mountainous mainland. We shivered in the pouring rain, reconciling ourselves to a second night at sea. In the afternoon the north wind returned, too late. It was a full-fledged "norther," the standard winter storm, confused by successive cold fronts. When the sun went down a full moon alternately shone and was hidden by swift, black clouds. By 8:30 p.m. we were twelve miles off the river mouth. We dropped sails, deployed the sea anchor, and drifted at .75 knots. We stripped off our raingear and squeezed into the cabin. Things were getting wet from a mysterious leak. We cuddled and warmed as best we could, rocking madly with the waves.

I slept but fortunately Ginny kept her eye on the GPS. She woke me at midnight. "Hey, we're drifting a lot faster now. Two knots," she said. I pulled in the sea anchor. It had split open, so I dropped the regular anchor and fifty feet of rode. Our drift slowed again.

When the sun came up on February 15, 2011, we were five miles off shore in a confused sea. The Rio Sico had four mouths. We sailed along them, south to north, just outside the breakers, standing tall, scrutinizing. All were blocked by the swells being generated by the norther. What now?

A lobster boat was anchored a half mile off the northernmost mouth so we went and talked to them. It had stacked canoes and bunks for a score of scuba-divers. The skipper said he lived in Palacios, the town inside the mouth. He would be coming and going because he was readying the *Miss Kaidy*, as she was named, for a trip to the reefs around Cabo Gracias a Dios. We anchored nearby and dozed fitfully until a wave filled the cockpit. After that I stayed in the cockpit to monitor the situation. The holding ground was good but the sea was high and killer surf lay to lee.

At 1:30 a twenty-five-foot launch with twin 200-horse Yamahas came up. They took us aboard, their boat bouncing crazily next to ours. In the transfer I fell in the water and Ginny banged her knee. The launch collected some lobster tails from the *Miss Kaidy* then returned to the bar, running fast between breaking waves. It was so easy for them! Once inside we were taken to a hotel where we napped, and were bitten by fleas. The storm picked up as we dined on the covered porch of the town's only restaurant. Would *Thurston* survive the tempest unattended?

The next morning the launch took us back out to *Thurston*. She was still there, but the tie on the mizzen sail had broken loose. The sail had flogged all night, ripping it and flinging out the battens. The sea was still too rough to tow her in.

By the third morning the swell had lessened so they took me out again. We connected a long tow line. I urged them to go slow because *Thurston's* stern tapers to a fine point and I was afraid high speed might

50

tow her under. They wisely ignored me. As before, they entered a bit faster than the breakers, staying in between and slowly gaining. In the unaccustomed speed *Thurston's* stern squatted until her flat bottom began to plane, whereafter she docilely followed the launch into the calm waters of the estuary. What a relief!

Palacios had a single dirt track with docks on one side and houses on the other. The village more or less marked the east limit of the Garifunas and the west limit of the Miskitos. Both are peoples of mixed African and Native American ancestry with languages that sprang up when the coming of the Europeans caused various peoples to collide. Yet the two tongues, and peoples, are very different. The Garifunas extended northwest into Belize. The Miskitos extended southeast into Nicaragua. During the time of English influence, from 1630 to 1860, Palacios was called the Black River Settlement. Englishmen lived and traded here in alliance with the Miskitos but left when Britain renounced her claims to the area.

The word Miskito, in reference to the people, is not derived from "mosquito." Whether "Mosquito Coast" refers to the people or the insect is unclear but also academic. Both are plentiful. The Hondurans call their portion of this coastline *La Mosquitia.*

Miss Kaidy's divers were Miskitos, her seamen mostly mestizos (mixed Indian and white). Throughout the day crewmembers assembled at the owner's dock in preparation for a return to their fishing grounds. They were drinking rum. One wanted to fight another, claiming he had said something improper to his woman. The others held them apart, laughing. Two got so drunk they had to be lowered onto the launch like sacks of potatoes.

By this time our hotel room and adjoining porch rail were festooned with drying bedding, clothes, and books. Our hotel sat on pilings and was plank-built in the shape of a U. The arms of the U projected out over the water. It had ten small rooms opening onto the U. The corridor around the U was open but roofed. There was one semifunctional bathroom, no electricity, no sign, no reception. Our door couldn't be closed all the way. This contributed to a scare late the second night when someone entered our room. Ginny sat up and yelled, "Hey!" The person mumbled something and walked away. He was probably just looking for a place to sleep.

Ginny with giant beetle, Palacios, Honduras
(while a little kid tries to take the headlamp from her pocket)

We found that the leak we had experienced during the crossing came from a crack in the mizzen mast step, which is a plastic tube. We scrounged a roll of gauze and wrapped it around the tube while saturating it with epoxy. We also needed sail repairs, a new sea anchor, and cash, all unavailable in Palacios, so we arranged for a ride to La Ceiba.

It was starting to get light at 5:30 a.m. when someone called out to us from a boat. We dropped from the porch into the boat, six feet below. They crossed the estuary to a site where people and gear were being loaded into four-wheel-drive pickup trucks. We were placed in the back of a Toyota Hilux short-bed along with three other adults, a child, a baby, and everyone's luggage. The track ran through palms and sea grapes by the beach, and occasionally on the beach itself, in which instances the truck ran in spurts to avoid waves crashing up to the jungle's edge.

We came to a minor river mouth. Via a pair of planks we drove onto a ferry consisting of plastic drums inside a planked frame. A motor launch moved the ferry to the other side. Four similar ferry crossings followed. We changed cars twice for reasons beyond our ken. To avoid pain we kept shifting position to the limited extent allowed us. When it started raining they pulled a tarp over us. The wind caused it to mold to our faces as we faced forward above the level of the cab. We missed not being able to see until Ginny noticed that there were tiny holes in the tarp. By placing a hole exactly over a pupil we could see ahead as if through a tiny tube! When a raindrop plugged the hole we tapped the tarp to clear it.

After a week back in La Ceiba we returned to Palacios by the same means. Our ninety-day visa and thirty-day extension were nearly expired yet we had another 140 windward miles to go to round Cabo Gracias a Dios. So on February 28 we sailed out the mouth, which by then had calmed down, and east into the wind along a flat, uninhabited coast. We easily made it to Brus Lagoon, but the following day it was nip and tuck whether we would reach the next refuge, the Rio Patuca, before dark. The tension was maddening. We fought for every inch of progress against the wind and current, constantly tacking, knowing that if we were late we would have to go at least five miles out to sea and sleep at sea anchor, which is not to sleep at all. The sun had set and the light was dimming when we started seeing sand bars and breakers. The mouth was too difficult to attempt in low light. Fortunately we passed a fisherman tending his net. I offered him five dollars worth of lempiras, the Honduran currency, to tow us in. He accepted.

The river was brown, the omnipresent foliage dark green. On the right bank was a town of wooden shacks. Some had once been painted, but all were now jungle-stained. Boardwalks spanned a couple of creeks. We pulled up in front of a big cross where people were gathered. A middle-aged black man introduced himself as their elected leader. "We are indigenous people here," he said. "We speak Miskito and Spanish too." There being no police force he insisted on assigning three men to watch over us during the night. Then he left.

"How much will I have to pay?" I asked the lead watchman. "Whatever you feel is right," he said. But discussion must have ensued during the night because at dawn he waded out to us and stood nervously erect. "That will be one hundred dollars, please." I gave him twelve dollars worth of lempiras and a lecture to the effect that even to a gringo a hundred dollars is a lot of money. He acquiesced. I paid the chief another fifteen dollars for a tow out the mouth, and we parted on good terms.

It was forty-five miles to the next refuge, a sandbar at the Barra de la Caratasca, that is, the entrance to the lagoon of that name. Again, we barely got there by dusk. Sailing between a pair of shipwrecks, we anchored in the lee of the sandbar. A campfire kindled far away on the other side of the mouth. We waded to the exposed sand and scampered about, delighted to have found a spot so fresh, open, and still. During the night hundreds of terns sang and whirled about.

In the morning we stopped at a naval post for inspection. While we waited a crowd of spotlessly dressed sailors carried two of their number on their shoulders to the end of the dock and threw them in with much laughter. "Initiates," a lieutenant said. Then we entered the vast lagoon containing Puerto Lempira, the district capital.

Preparing to go ashore, Puerto Lempira, Honduras

. . . AND PANAMA,

The town was eight miles inside. It had dirt streets and a long, broken dock. Freighters were unloading barrels of fuel into the water to be towed ashore. We got laundry done, bought drinking water, and secured a clearance for Puerto Cabezas, Nicaragua. Then, for privacy, we anchored in a lagoon behind the town.

In the middle of the night shooting started. For hours a battle raged around the town: single shots, automatic fire, and explosions. Fiery missiles flew in shallow arcs, high in the dark sky. To me it seemed too far away to worry about. "Must be army exercises," I said and fell back asleep. Ginny didn't buy it. She remained awake, afraid we would be struck by stray bullets. In the morning the town's shopkeepers complained that rival mafias had been fighting. Three were dead. *La Mosquitia* was a major drug transshipment zone.

The Navy warned us not to hug the coast. The only alternative was to follow an intermittent arc of reefs and cayes that wraps around Cabo Gracias a Dios. Most were about forty miles offshore and the distance from the first island to the last was 150 miles. The closest were the Cayos Vivorillos, northeast of Barra de la Caratasca. In preparation for the crossing we spent a second night behind the sandbar.

A half hour before light we started sailing out the mouth. The wind died, and before we could set up the rowing station a current carried us into the breakers to our left. The bow shot up in a splash of spray. Adrenaline pumping, I pulled us back into the channel.

The sun came up as land receded. For seven hours we rowed with some assist from the sails. We traded off. The party not rowing steered with lines running back to the tiller. The steerer´s job was almost as tedious as the rower´s because the hatch had to stay shut, that being our policy whenever sail was up. Without the companionway to dangle one´s legs in the steerer had to scrunch up on the scrap of deck between the rower and the companionway. Finally the breeze grew. We put the oars down and trimmed the sheets.

"There, trees, eight miles away!" A current was pulling us left. We compensated, finally entering the island's lee. It and several other specks of loose coral rock, lightly vegetated, formed a crescent-shaped chain. Two yachts lay at anchor within the crescent. We anchored by a huge stack of wooden lobster traps and slept.

It was only twenty miles from there to Cayo Cocorocuma, but

due to adverse wind and current the passage took eleven hours. The island was a base for lobster divers. Then we sailed to Logwood Caye, which must have been washed away in a hurricane because only a coral reef remained. We anchored in exposed water and bounced around all night.

March 9 was similar: a long crossing in hope of an island to hide behind. Alas, Edinburgh Caye has also sunk beneath the waves. But enough daylight remained that we might reach Cayo Muerto. By this time we had followed the crescent of islands to where the bearings between them were more south than east. Since the wind came from the east, our boat speed had increased with each crossing, and now we were enjoying almost a beam reach. But the sun was sinking and still we saw no land. We stared nervously into the horizon. A sail off the port bow distracted us, then others. What were sailboats doing along a coast avoided by yachts? We forced ourselves to concentrate on the supposed island. It might be another coral patch. Then Ginny spied a couple of dead trees stranded on a shoal. There was no island, no coral, just eel grass! Cayo Muerto was in fact dead. Its lee provided excellent shelter nonetheless.

In the morning a fleet of sailboats approached, the same we had seen the evening before. One drew up onto the shoal. It was a wooden double-ender, about thirty-six feet long, with a crew of fourteen wiry young men, mainly Miskitos. It had a tree-trunk mast, a gaffed mainsail, and a jib on a long bowsprit. There was no deck or floor, just thwarts and sloshing bilges. *"Agua!"* one said, holding up an empty jug. We gave him two liters. Others boats pulled up. They asked questions and sounded us out for generosity. They made us nervous. We had been warned about piracy in Nicaragua. Upon understanding that we were Americans one sidled up to me and confessed a fascination for World War II history. I thought this odd in a person seemingly so rooted in the here and now of a Latin American backwater. But he was sincere so I told him how my father and uncle had fought in that war. This impressed him deeply.

We continued south between large mangrove islands. The weather was mild so we continued into the night. At 10:00 p.m., ten miles from Puerto Cabezas, we dropped the sails and paid out the sea anchor we'd had made in La Ceiba. It was a large truncated cone made of canvas. It worked fine, but the weather deteriorated. Heavy rain came, twenty knots of wind, horrible motion. Another norther had arrived. A wave crashed through a side window, soaking our blanket. Sleep was impossible. It was March 11, 2011.

After an endless night we sailed into Puerto Cabezas, Nicaragua. It sat on a bluff. It had no harbor, just a long, exposed pier. It was hard to dock without smashing against it. Naval personnel searched *Thurston,* then a taxi took us to the immigration office. An official in a crisp white shirt with blue shoulder boards perused our passports.

"We have a problem," he said. "You have already exceeded your ninety days allowance in Central America. We can't allow you into Nicaragua." We knew that Guatemala, Honduras, Nicaragua, and El Salvador had agreed to limit tourist stays to ninety days within the four countries as a whole, but the restriction wasn't enforced in Honduras. We had hoped it wouldn't be in Nicaragua, either. For an hour he scolded and scared us, then offered us thirty days in exchange for $300 in "fines." We paid, hoping it would be enough time to reach Costa Rica.

Fishing sloops in Puerto Cabezas, Nicaragua

We found an eight-dollar hotel room and a grocery store. At midnight I checked on *Thurston*. On the dock I passed a line of black plastic bundles. They were Miskito fishermen ready to depart in open sailboats like those we had seen at Cayo Muerto. They slept on the dock and rolled themselves up in plastic sheeting when it rained!

Getting back aboard the next morning was like jumping from a fence onto a bucking bronco with a week's worth of groceries! Our clearance was for Bluefields, the biggest town on the Caribbean coast of Nicaragua.

The shore was now low jungle. The first night we slept at Rio Huahua, where the village chief paddled out with an empty container to beg for gasoline. He gave up when he saw we had no motor. The second day we reached Prinzapolka, an oddly-named Miskito village. At our third stop, La Barra del Rio Grande, the residents spoke Creole English and listened to Country Western music. In the evening they strolled the concrete walkway that ran through the village while Brahman cattle wandered contentedly in the marshy flats. The final night we spent behind one the Cayos Perlas, a cluster of islands ten miles offshore. We sailed the final forty-four miles at speeds of up to nine knots! Rounding Cabo Gracias a Dios had put us back on a favorable angle to the trade winds.

On March 18 we rounded a tall promontory, entered a bay full of mothballed shrimp boats, and pulled up at a dock to report our arrival. I found the port captain in an office on top of the hill. He was a short, officious man. "Bluefields is across the bay. This is El Bluff. We are a separate district. I'll have to give you a new clearance for Bluefields."

I knew what that meant. "No way! I already paid twenty-five dollars for a *zarpe* for Bluefields. I'm not buying another one from you!"

"You've come ashore. You're under my jurisdiction now. You need a new *zarpe*."

I snatched my *zarpe* from his hand. "Give me an armed guard and search the boat if you like but I'm not buying another *zarpe*."

The port captain was aghast. "Calm down!" he said, "show me some respect!" But he ended up doing as I suggested. *Thurston* was searched and we were given another paper, but at least we didn't have to pay again.

Free at last, we crossed the lagoon to Bluefields proper. The shore was studded with wrecks and broken pilings. At the head of a cove surrounded by slums we found a creek lined with cargo-carrying dugouts. We laid the masts on deck to duck under a low bridge. I sat on the bow paddling and Ginny steered while the creek meandered through hilly countryside. We came to a grassy bend where fiberglass launches had been pulled up for repair next to a house of corrugated steel. I approached a tall, snaggle-toothed black man.

"Hello! Can we keep our boat here a few days? I can pay you 100 cordobas (five dollars) a day for security."

"Sure, mon," he said in Creole English. "You be fine here. My name Daniel but they calls me Mandingo."

We tied to trees and set up the awning. The bridge we had squeezed under was fifteen minutes away on foot. The city sloped down to a crowded waterfront. The public market was a smoke-smeared cavern full of ghastly and intriguing smells. The stall-keepers minded piles of yucca, pineapples, and shrimps. The cooks were grizzled women with head wraps, long dresses, and tired grins. We ate lunch at a crude bench then found an internet place. We had a lot of writing and research to do.

Each evening upon our return from town I gave Mandingo another hundred cordobas. On day four another fellow approached me, a skinny mestizo often seen whacking the grass with a machete. "I'm the caretaker here, not Mandingo!" he said, twitching nervously. "Why is he getting the money, not me?"

"I thought Mandingo was the owner!" I said.

"Mandingo doesn't even live here! My brother is the owner. I'm the caretaker!"

"Can't you work it out among yourselves?" I asked, but Skinny Man (as I thought of him) steered clear of Mandingo.

He hurried up to me again the next day, in obvious anguish. "I watch this place! You should pay me!"

"How should I know who to pay? I need to talk to your brother!"

"That's him right there." Skinny Man timidly indicated a chubby fellow sitting under a tree next to Mandingo.

I introduced myself. "Hello! There seems to be some confusion as to who I should pay the hundred cordobas per day to. I don't want to cause any trouble."

"*Tranquilo, amigo.* That is not your problem. Let them work it out!"

"Yes, don't worry. I'll share it with him," Mandingo assured.

"Okay, great. But if you don't mind, today I'll give the money to him." I walked over and handed Skinny Man the bill. He smiled feebly. I paid Mandingo one day, Skinny Man the next until March 31, when we got a clearance for Limón, Costa Rica with stopover in San Juan del Norte.

Waterfront slum, Bluefields, Nicaragua

We then sailed down a coast sprinkled with tall, rocky islands to Monkey Bay, a calm cove with a sandy beach. Here we found twenty or so rustic, elevated dwellings interspersed with trees from which hung nests like long, droopy sacks. Black birds with bright yellow tails inhabited these nests, in a bird community overlapping the human community. At one of the houses we found 27-year-old heavyweight boxer Evans Quinn, whom we had met in Bluefields. Evans was on a break between fights in such locales as Germany, Australia, and the U.S. He was hospitable, almost fawning. Finally he worked himself up to his proposition. "You be my manager," he urged! "We'll make millions when I become world champion." I gratefully declined. That would have been an interesting outcome, but it was rather far afield.

Our next stop was Rio Maiz, which issues from a vast wilderness. We anchored in wading depth beside a village. The people spoke Creole and subsisted by fishing and cultivating small plots in the forest. While Ginny and I relaxed in the cockpit with the awning up the local kids stood around *Thurston* with their torsos inside the awning, watching us like we were television. There were no thoroughfares, but the beach was an endless promenade. The sand was dark grey and soft as powder.

Our next refuge would be the Rio San Juan at the border with Costa Rica. We had to stop there to get Nicaraguan exit stamps in our passports. Our chart showed a complicated pattern of mouths, channels, and lagoons. Google Earth's satellite image, which we had saved onto our laptop in Bluefields, showed a different pattern. Our acquaintances in Rio Maiz could only tell us that the San Juan mouth was dangerous and that after entering we should turn right to reach the town.

We accepted a tow out the mouth, which was much rougher now. We sailed to where the Rio San Juan's mouth should have been per the GPS but saw no opening. We found a mouth a half mile further south, and anchored outside the surf. I swam in. A small river, upon reaching the shore, turned left, parallel to the beach. A sand spit separated the river from the ocean for 200 yards, then tapered to nothing as fresh water mixed with salt. The breakers were six feet tall. Meanwhile a squall came. Ginny, thrashing at anchor, waited anxiously. When I returned we decided to proceed to Costa Rica without exit stamps. We weighed anchor and sailed to a Nicaraguan military boat anchored a mile offshore. I grabbed our handheld VHF radio and tried to raise the boat, intending to ask them about the bar of the Rio Colorado, ten miles south. At first the conversation was in Spanish, roughly as follows:

"Small sailboat to military boat."

"Wait, let me connect you." After a pause another voice said,

"Did you want to enter the mouth?"

"It looks too dangerous."

"A boat can tow you. It won't be dangerous."

"How much will it cost?"

Switching to English my interlocutor answered, "Nothing. It will be free."

I conferred with Ginny. "Okay, we'll take a tow."

"Wait for a white launch."

Ten minutes later a *panga* (the local open boat) with two men arrived. We passed them our longest, heaviest line. They towed us not to the river mouth we had found, but to where the mouth was supposed to have been per the GPS. There was still no sign of an opening, just continuous surf, yet they proceeded at high speed! At the last instant the motorman cut his throttle, veered left, and shot up over a breaker. The man in the bow flew six feet into the air then landed with a thump in the bottom of the boat. They swerved right, then left again. We followed helplessly two hundred feet behind, narrowly missing breakers. Suddenly a river mouth appeared! It was like the one I had swam to in that the river at its end ran parallel to the coast, separated from the ocean by a sand spit. The sand spit had blended in with the steep beach behind. We followed the river as it paralleled the shore, then turned inland, then teed into a linear lagoon. We turned right and soon stopped at a dock on the left bank. A short, white-skinned, grey-haired man awaited us. He was smiling and singing something.

"Was it you I talked to on the VHF?" I asked.

"Yes, welcome! My name is Gustavo Peterson."

"Is this a military installation? Do you want to see our papers?"

"Oh, no. This business belongs to Eden Pastora. We keep the river dredged." He looked bemused. "Say, can you help me with this song? I have the words here but I can't remember the melody very well."

He showed me a paper. It was the words to My Way, popularized by Frank Sinatra. I helped him sang it, the final line being, "And I did it myyyy wayyyy!"

"Thank you," he said. "It's good to remember America. As for Eden Pastora . . ." Gustavo explained that the owner was the Sandinista *Comandante Uno* while Somoza was being overthrown in the 1970s. Then he became a Contra leader *against* the Sandinistas in the 1980s because he didn't like how socialism turned out. When the Contras lost he eventually reconciled with Daniel Ortega and rejoined his government. So he had switched sides twice, yet was still respected.

"Did you fight too?" I asked.

"Yes. I was a *Somozista* during the insurgency, so my side fought against Pastora. But we both became Contras. I trained in Texas and Georgia. The CIA gave me weapons. In fact, I led the attack on this town, or the previous town, actually. After we burned Greytown the residents fled to Costa Rica. When they returned they rebuilt here, four miles away from the original place."

Eden Pastora's installation lay at the entrance to the town of San Juan del Norte, which we now explored. It consisted of a large grid of concrete walkways, often elevated above the marshy terrain. The walkways accessed tidy new homes and government buildings. In the center was a cobble-paved street without cars. A baseball tournament was beginning. Rival teams were arriving by boat from surrounding communities. Each team wore a distinct colorful uniform.

Ball teams in San Juan del Norte, Nicaragua

At the tourist office we studied documents about the Rio San Juan. It drains Lago Nicaragua, the huge lake that occupies the center of the country. The Spanish founded San Juan del Norte in 1539 in a natural harbor at the river's mouth. In the 1700s pirates, British troops, and Miskito Indians attacked the Spanish forts along the river. In the 1800s it was part of the Miskito Kingdom. The British renamed it Greytown for the governor of Jamaica, whose job it was to crown the Miskito kings.

In 1849 San Juan del Norte became the eastern terminus of a transport company owned by Cornelius Vanderbilt that carried California Gold Rush "49ers" from the Atlantic coast to the Pacific. They started building a trans-isthmus canal parallel to the river but the Panama Canal got built instead. In 1854 the U.S. Navy sloop *Cyane* bombarded the town, supposedly in retaliation against an abuse of American citizens. In 1855 American soldier-of-fortune William Walker declared himself President of Nicaragua. Guatemala, Honduras, and Costa Rica helped repel the invading gringos. Walker died before a firing squad. Around then the river shifted most of its flow to the Rio Colorado mouth, in Costa Rica. The San Juan mouth silted in. Greytown Harbor became a lake. Nicaragua no longer controlled a navigable route to the Atlantic. The mouth I had swam to was that of the Rio San Juan. It connects with the Rio Indio, whose mouth we had entered.

We went with Gustavo to see what remained of Greytown. A launch took us though narrow, hyacinth-clogged channels to a landing where men were unloading sand with shovels and buckets. Sentries checked us in. The old town site was now an army camp. They were building a new airstrip. Next to the area being leveled were four cemeteries: British, Catholic, Masonic, and American. Most of the interred had died in the 1800s. Antique bottles and iron artifacts lay in heaps.

Gustavo was discretely nostalgic. "This is my first time back since the battle," he said out of hearing of the soldiers. "I don't tell the people here about my involvement. We killed a hundred of them. We attacked from that direction," he said pointing east. We stopped beside a brick foundation. A sign said it had been the Catholic church. Gustavo stared. "That's funny, we didn't burn the church," he said. But it too was now gone.

After three days we got our exit papers and accepted a tow back out the mouth. At the point of no return the skipper hesitated while studying the six-foot tall breakers. Deciding to go, he powered seaward. *Thurston* slammed into the first wall of foam, drenching us and filling the cockpit. We crested another and another until we reached open sea, relieved to have again crossed the bar successfully. We retrieved our line. We were alone again.

The heavy swell that had caused the dangerous surf at the mouth of the Rio Indio persisted as we sailed south, sealing off the upcoming river mouths. We would have to continue to Puerto Limón, Costa Rica. It was seventy miles away, so we would have to spend at least one night at sea.

We had little wind until a rainsquall hit, then it slowly built to twenty or twenty-five knots. Sea Pearls have no keel, so you have to reef them "early and often." Fortunately they are easy to reef, allowing you to employ the optimum amount of sail area at all times. You disengage a tab at the gooseneck, unclip the vang, uncleat the outhaul, rotate the mast by hand the desired number of turns, then refasten the tab, vang, and outhaul. The main, being bigger, requires more reefing than the mizzen. In this instance, as the wind built we put two rolls in the main, then two more, then two in the mizzen, then a fifth and six in the main, then a third and fourth in the mizzen. With about two thirds of our Dacron now furled the heel was manageable but the waves were scary because of the underlying swells. Then the wind died. We rolled the sails back out in reverse sequence until we were becalmed. The sea remained too rough to row. We sat for hours wishing we had stayed in San Juan del Norte.

After dark another squall hit. Clipped in now, we passed through the same stages. The wind stopped again, but not the rain. Our worn foul weather gear no longer kept us dry. At 10:00 p.m., cold and tired, we dropped the sails and deployed the sea anchor. *Thurston's* narrow beam and round bilges caused her to roll a lot, but the night was calm. We slept fairly well, twenty miles offshore.

In the morning the sea was glassy but for the swells. We rowed most of the day, averaging about 2.5 knots, taking turns to minimize blisters. As the passage's second night stole over the silver wastes the lights of Limón became visible. They slowly became distinguishable as ships, docks, and buildings. At 10:00 p.m. we rounded a point and tied to a buoy. We were in Costa Rica! It was April 8, 2011.

In the morning we found the port captain and the immigration and customs offices. A Holland America cruise ship was in port. Its passengers thronged a big circus tent set up on the dock for tourist shopping. We didn't see them in the streets, though. There, Spanish and Creole English intermingled and the currency was *colones,* five hundred to the dollar.

In need of a better mooring we explored a small river at the head of the harbor. It was a many-fingered mangrove estuary. A slum called Cienegitas sprawled though its muddy flats. Everyone said to stay away, but it was the only protected water near town. The houses were rotting and crooked. Techno-reggae blared from speakers. Vultures thrust their scaly heads into piles of garbage. We found a compound containing a house and boat yard. The owner agreed to host us for $5 per day. After hanging our gear up to dry we walked downtown, running where it looked most dangerous. This was not paranoia; a taxi driver was murdered during our stay there. Downtown was relatively safe, and its fruit and vegetable stands were well-stocked. Every day I ate three kilos of mangos.

On our fourth day in Limón we visited an outlying area on the other side of town. There were no houses, just a school and some docks. We were walking along a gravel road and had just crossed a bridge over a canal. We were engrossed in conversation. Suddenly a rearward tug threw me off balance. I wheeled around. Teenage boys were stealing our daypacks! One yelled savagely while waving a kitchen knife an arm's length away. Another tried to yank Ginny's pack away while brandishing a jagged rock. Somebody behind me knocked my feet out from under me. Sprawled on the ground, I let them take my wallet and daypack. "Ginny, give up!" I yelled, but she couldn't hear me, so furiously was she was screaming and swearing. I'd had two on me, and they were adept. She gave her assailant more trouble. The boy hesitated to hit her with the rock, and when he did he didn't use his full force. Finally he jerked the pack away. Instantly they melted into the woods. Ginny had blood trickling down her face from a cut on her scalp. We found some rusty car parts on the side of the road to serve as weapons and followed them. Fifty yards in we found our gear.

They had kept our digital camera, cell phone, and $150, but had left our passports. We remembered that they were wet and barefoot, and that while crossing the bridge we had seen boys swimming in the canal. They must have promptly climbed the bank and snuck up behind us, their bare feet muffling their footsteps. They'd caught us totally off guard.

Unwilling that this should ruin our stay in Costa Rica, we took a bus to San Jose, the capital. We got an air-conditioned room and explored. The place was bursting with pastry shops! After five days there we tried Cartago, a smaller town from which we took hikes in the mountains. There we were nearly robbed again.

We had gone on a long scramble in the foothills and were walking back to town on a country road. A taxi cab passed going the same way. After continuing a short distance he turned around and came back. Stopping alongside, the driver pointed to a car pulled over a hundred yards ahead. "Those men are going to assault you!" he said. "Get in!"

"How do you know that?" I asked.

"I just know. I saw one of them make his gun ready, like this." He pantomimed pulling the slide back on a semi-auto pistol, feeding a bullet into the chamber. "Don't worry, I won't charge anything." We gratefully accepted.

As we drove past the car, four men inside it were watching. One yelled out, "We weren't going to hurt you!" The taxi driver drove into Cartago and dropped us off at our hotel without further discussion. His interpretation of their intentions was credible.

We decided we stood out too much, so I bought a packet of Miss Clairol and dyed my hair black. Now I looked like Ozzy Osborne. Meanwhile Ginny bought a tight pair of pants to better blend in with the sexy Costa Rican women. "Being crime victims has made us younger!" we joked. Beneath the bravado we were a bit rattled.

Back at the coast we got a clearance, and on April 27 left for Panama. Beyond Limón the shoreline became an archipelago of hilly islands and shallow bays. Mangrove lined the shores, and howler monkeys filled the tree tops with their long, baffling intonations. After months of scanty protection these sheltered waters were delightful. The center of activity was Bocas del Toro, a yachting Mecca accessible only by boat.

Ginny gets back to her roots in Bocas del Toro, Panama.

It was time to ponder our route forward. We had begun the voyage to access the Caribbean's best snorkeling sites. We had done so, but the voyage itself had won us over, addicting us to its freedom and adventure. We wanted to keep going! On my part there was also a strange question of age intervals, or self-divination. It goes like this.

My first limitless travel, in Europe, Asia, and Morocco, started when I was eighteen years old. My second, the three years in *Squeak,* started when the wanderlust again became irresible, at age thirty-six. I was then twice as old. When I realized that I had experienced two eighteen-year cycles I wondered if that was significant, but I didn't think much of it. Then, at age fifty-four, I found myself traveling with Ginny on the truck-and-canoe trip that led to the current voyage. Another eighteen-year interval! The natural periodicity of my wanderlust! The five years referred to in the title of this book exclude the initial pickup-truck travel, but it was all one adventure. I decided that I was still engrossed in a third cycle. My preference was to again travel as long as the wanderlust lasted.

Ginny had no objection. For her our departure in 2007 was an escape from boredom and stagnation. Our lifestyle suited her to a tee. The constant change and open-endedness felt natural. This was her first limitless travel, and she was blossoming like a potent flower.

We would keep going, but where? We decided, tentatively, to cross the Isthmus of Panama and continue south along the Pacific coast of South America, as I had done in 1991. Thus we could avoid countering the trade winds.

At the same time we had another consideration. We had three reasons to go back home first. One, the rainy season was now starting, and I knew from experience that the Pacific coast of Colombia is inhospitable in those months. Two, we'd been gone for two years and loose ends had accumulated. And three, my dad had developed a serious heart ailment. It might be my last chance to see him. So we got return trip tickets to the States. The Bocas Marina agreed to watch *Thurston* for a nominal fee. We sat her on the lawn next to their office and packed up.

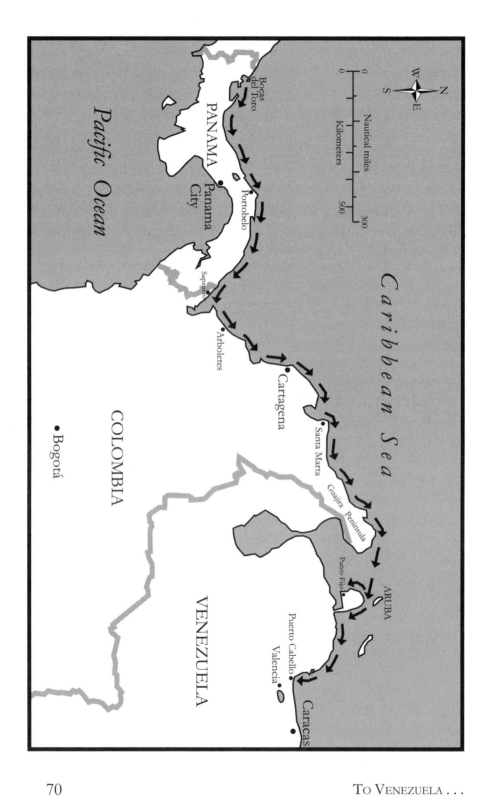

Chapter 4
TO VENEZUELA WITH A SECRET WEAPON

It took two days to reach Panama City by boat and bus. From there we flew to Miami, arriving on May 3. We drove a rental car to Pine Island, Florida, where we retrieved our Isuzu pickup. It was fun to be on the road again in our little truck. How *nice* America is! Clean bathrooms! Showers with *hot* water! Water fountains with *cold* water! The supermarkets abounded with fresh, delicious foods.

On our way back to Washington State we attended the annual Cedar Key Small Boat Meet in Cedar Key, Florida. We also visited friends Larry and Karen in Atlanta and Lena and Jesse in St. Louis. Back home we lived at my parents' house in Bremerton, taking care of loose ends and getting ready for the next phase of our voyage.

At the end of the summer we drove back to Larry's, parked the truck there, and flew back to Panama. In the capital city we picked up a new Honda two-horsepower outboard motor we had arranged to purchase. It was four-stroke, air-cooled. It weighted only twenty-eight pounds! Going motorless thus far had certainly developed our sailing and rowing skills. But Honduras had been excruciating due to the headwinds and lack of harbors. Now we had boxed ourselves into a corner by sailing to the southwest extremity of the Caribbean because the winds come from the northeast. Everything else in the Caribbean would be to windward.

Returning to Bocas del Toro on September 9, after a four-month interlude, we found *Thurston* in good shape. We installed the motor mount and a new set of sails. It was hot and buggy at the marina, but we defended ourselves with an array of creams, nets, and smoke coils.

To get to town we either paddled our inflatable kayak or walked around an intervening bay through the mangroves, which smelled of ammonia from decomposing vegetation.

For four days we cruised the nearby islands while trying out the new installations. Our favorite nocturnal tie-up was in a clear stream with a forest to one side and on the other a field grazed by Brahman cattle. It rained all night, and the fresh water streaming over and under us smelled clean after so much salt. We finally saw sloths overhead! They have long, coarse fur (they say an entire ecosystem lives within it!) and don't move much. The sloth is Ginny's totem; they both excel at leisure. "It's a spiritual thing," quipped Ginny.

Overnighting up a stream near Bocas del Toro, Panama

The rainy season, which so complicates tropical travel, was ending. Our equipment was in order. On October 2, 2011, we resumed our voyage, but not Plan A. We had changed our minds. Rather than cross over to the Pacific we decided to follow the north coast of South America eastward. That would be against the wind, but our new motor would allow us to power straight to windward rather than zigzag. We had bought charts of the Caribbean coasts of Panama, Colombia, and Venezuela. We would make another route decision in Venezuela.

Leaving the inland sea we sailed to a big island called Escudo de Veraguas. A few indigenous families lived there. They were shy toward us. After that the coastline offered little protection other than small river mouths. Fortunately, the swells were small so we could enter anything with a foot of depth.

The Isthmus of Panama is narrow, tall, and heavily forested. Most of the villages are inaccessible except by boat. We stayed in a friendly place called Calovebora a couple of days. It had two stores, a school, and a quaint ritual of late afternoon bathing. We lathered up in the river with the ladies and their laundry. Meanwhile the children splashed around the tethered *pangas*, taking special delight in diving from the gunwales into the water. The men tinkered with outboard motors. From the village various trails radiated out to coastal landholdings where the people had erected fences to keep cattle from falling off the seaside cliffs.

Our next stop was the Rio Belén, where Christopher Columbus had to abandon a ship on one of his voyages. After rowing upstream two miles we pulled over at a native hamlet consisting of six primitive houses spread over some cleared hills. They had cattle, pigs, goats, chickens, and dogs. They kept their dugouts in a little tributary ravine. With their permission we parked there also. The many curious children took advantage of the ravine's steep banks and climbing trees to perch themselves overhead and comment upon our every move. They gave us plantains to eat, and a strange wild fruit that is like a large bean-pod with a woody brown husk. The edible part is a sugary white fur around the hard black beans. We shared our cookies, the best thing we had.

We also explored the Rio Chagres, a wild river with no sign of people along the banks until we reached Gatun Dam, six miles up. There the river is impounded to power the locks in the Panama Canal.

We sailed past the busy Panama Canal entrance and on to Portobelo, a day's travel away. At Portobelo the Spaniards used to load their treasure fleets with silver and gold. The ancient harbor forts still stand, their cupola-capped sentry booths intact, cannons protruding

Overnighting with an Indian family on the Rio Belén, Panama

Kids overhead, same location

To Venezuela . . .

from the embrasures. The town is small but boasts a cathedral in which stands a statue of the Black Christ. Many worship him, often traveling great distances to do so. Thirty-odd sailboats from all over the world lay at anchor.

We stayed for six days, including a side trip to Panama City. There we went in search of a certain upholsterer whose name and address we'd gotten from a web site. We took a slow, crowded bus to the approximate area. There were no street name signs or address numbers so we could only ask around. When we finally found the place it turned out that he had moved six years earlier! By this time we had been walking for two hours so we persuaded someone to phone the upholsterer. Bless his heart, he came and picked us up in his car! He then drove us all over the city obtaining the correct cloth, thread, and needles to repair our awning, for he seemed to have nothing on hand. His shop was a converted house, very messy. At 9:00 p.m. he finished the repair, cleared off a couple of couches for us to sleep on, and left. In the morning we locked the door per his instructions, walked to a bus stop, and commenced the grueling return to our boat.

Panama is four hundred nautical miles from west to east. Portobelo was the halfway point. From there we passed through the San Blas Islands, land of the Kuna Indians. The coastline remained road-less. Some of the islands were hilly, others mangrove-rimmed. The sonorous howling of monkeys was never far distant. Birds made many strange cries. The Kunas maintained a traditional life-style, some on islands, others on the mainland. Many of the women still dressed in their colorful traditional garb. Their homes were of stick and thatch, their boats were motorless dugouts. They lived in dense villages, not in scattered homes. In one bay we passed a clump of six low isles, all entirely urbanized, like a Kuna Venice.

We mostly slept undetected in out-of-the-way places, but one evening our luck failed us. We pulled into a small river mouth a half mile from a village. The males immediately ran over to us. They spoke excitedly in Kuna among themselves, Spanish with us. One said we had violated their law by entering the river. If we didn't pay a fine of fifty dollars (Panama used U.S. currency) they would call the *policia nacional.* "No, a hundred dollars!" cried another. Finally the *Autoridad Maxima* (Maximum Authority) arrived, the oldest man in the village.

He was a small, slender man with smooth, honey-colored skin and cataract-covered eyes. He wore faded brown slacks and an old Tyrolean hat with a little feather. Perhaps due to blindness it took him a while to get his bearings. Finally he rendered his verdict. "One hundred fifty dollars!" Everyone laughed, for the people were jolly as well as mildly hostile.

After various defenses I hit on a proposal. "Okay, we will leave at once and sleep in front of your village. Whoever wants to can come with us so you know we won't escape. In the morning the *policia nacional* can come and sort it out."

This suggestion seemed to deflate them, perhaps because they didn't really want to involve the police. However, a ride in this strange and wonderful boat was not to be scorned, so five, including the *Autoridad Maxima,* climbed aboard. The latter sat on a side deck tapping this and that to see what it was made of. The others laughed and chattered. I rowed to the village. We anchored bow to shore, stern to sea. The surge was mild enough. I waded ashore and interacted with the masses. Everyone crowded in close. Fines were no longer mentioned. The schoolteacher taught me the Kuna word for "alright:" *"Neuti."*

"Neuti?" I asked the people to my left. *"Neuti?"* I asked to my right. *"Neuti,"* they said, the women smiling shyly. They wore bright, hand-crafted clothing with leggings like stacked beads. We retired and left early in the morning.

A south wind blew over the mountains in eddies and gusts, always too much wind or not enough. We now saw a new species of coastal freighter: clunky wooden double-enders from Colombia. A friendly mass of porpoises led us to a towering green mountain which tapered to a point called Cabo Tiburón: we had reached Colombia! Past the cape was a steep-sided cove in which nestled Sapzurro, a village catering to Colombian tourists. From there a trail led through hills to Capurganá, which lacked a harbor but was larger. We hiked there to officially enter the new country.

Sapzurro lay on the flank of the rainforest spine that joins Central and South America. We had now to leave Central America and get as far east as possible before the stronger dry-season winds arrived in December or January. According to the pilot charts Colombia has the biggest waves in the Caribbean. Trinidad, at the southeast corner of the sea, was 1,500 miles away. Refuges are few and the wind would be contrary, so we approached this coast somberly.

It had been a challenge to find places to stow the gas tank, oil, Baja fuel filter, and other motoring accessories. Like most people, Ginny is averse to the smell of gas, so everything that came into contact with it had to be washed with soap and water and wiped down with vinegar. These exigencies aside, the outboard motor was working well. It greatly boosted our range to windward. It would also allow us to ascend major rivers, but that lay in the future.

We had developed a policy for when to sail, row, and motor. If we could sail to our destination without tacking that's what we did. In Panama we'd had fair winds three quarters of the time, but that would soon change. In calms we rowed, but those too would disappear as the season progressed. More and more our route would be straight into the wind, obliging us to motor. Motoring felt like cheating, but it was fun and economical. From Bocas del Toro to Sapsurro we had used only two and a half gallons of gasoline! In such small quantities the cost was not a concern.

Ginny and I are minimalists, but what does that mean when you are on a voyage? Wouldn't it be more minimalistic just to stay home? My thinking on this was furthered one day while I was promoting *Three Years in a 12-Foot Boat*. I and another author were guests on a CBC radio talk show. The other guest had just written a book about extreme outdoor challenges. His thesis was that due to modern technology the only remaining challenges are those in which the adventurer purposely makes it harder, such as by climbing without oxygen or, in my case, sailing in a ridiculously small boat. (The host had cleverly added me to the program to illustrate the other guy's point.) "But that doesn't ring true with me," I said. "I didn't make my boat small in order to increase the challenge. I am an ecologist and a minimalist. I don't burn a lot of fossil fuel or live in a big house. I just carried that philosophy over into my adventuring." In other words, various motives might explain a decision to do something the hard way. Pilgrimages, for example, entail hardship. Taking a bus to Santiago de Compostela isn't the same as walking the Camino de Santiago. Ginny and I honored the nature we sailed through, minimized our impact, and found the compromise between purism and pragmatism that suited us.

I had briefly visited the Gulf of Uraba during my three-year voyage. It is shallow and extremely muddy due to the huge Atrato River flowing into it. The region is hot, humid, and primitive. From Sapzurro we motored east across the gulf's entrance, fighting the wind and a north-setting current. Carpets of water hyacinth flowed past, from right to left. On the other side we sheltered in a vast mangrove lagoon, then continued northeast.

The Caribbean coast of Colombia was low, rising to assorted hills, and relatively dry. On those distant uplands we saw scrubby woods, rarely any roads or buildings. Our second refuge was behind a man-made breakwater in the town of Arboletes. The beach was crowded with kids playing soccer and men drinking beer under thatched roofs. The town on top of the bluff provided us with produce, bread, and internet service. No one paid us any attention.

In each of the following days we arrived at a different set of low offshore islets. Rainstorms engulfed us: grey cloud banks, then squalls of wind, then lightning and torrential rain until we emerged on the far side of the storm. On the sixth day we entered Cartagena's vast outer harbor, a place of shipping and industry. From there we passed into the historic inner harbor.

In colonial times Cartagena was the principal port for ships arriving from Spain. To protect it the Spaniards built fortifications like those we had seen in Portobelo, but more extensive. The Walled City contained hundreds of blocks of picturesquely dilapidated architecture, well appreciated by tourists. We anchored among yachts in the inner harbor, but there were too many wakes, so we moved to a place where local passenger boats were parked. We paid six dollars a day for the calmer water, security, and convenience of being able to wade to shore. We were sometimes woken in the dead of night by men paddling past in canoes while vigorously flailing the water with long poles, presumably scaring fish into nets.

Affluent neighborhoods abut the Walled City, but the bulk of modern Cartagena lays further inland. Here dust and vehicles choked the streets. Chaotic markets stretched block upon block. Music and hawking spiels blared from speakers. We walked the shady side of streets and detained our breathing to avoid fumes. From a pile of garbage Ginny selected a hefty stick forty inches long. When new it had been lathed to a decorative shape, perhaps as a spindle in a staircase. When the staircase was demolished the spindle was discarded. It fit Ginny's hand nicely, so she carried it as a club. In good neighborhoods she tucked it unobtrusively behind her backpack. In bad ones she swung it like a billy club. I did not discourage her, having been mugged myself in Cartagena in 1973. On the contrary, while Ginny menaced with her cudgel I often openly toyed with my fist-sized folding knife. We were hard-asses!

One day, while we were walking in a wealthy neighborhood adjoining the yacht anchorage, we passed a beggarly man carrying a big duffle bag full of junk. As he passed he grumbled, *"Eso es mi palo!"* (That's my stick!) but made no attempt to retake it. As he receded down the sidewalk we harkened back to the pile from which Ginny had picked up the stick. Come to think of it, it had looked tended, as if articles of not-quite-zero value were placed there intentionally. We surmised that the junk man lacked a junk yard so he left articles here and there, let people know they were his, and relied on the honor system to eventually gain some benefit from them. Sorry junk man! We didn't know!

Our stay in Cartagena coincided with the city's 200th Independence Day celebration. For several days there were carnival parades. There were tiger women, and men in white tuxedos with pink hairdos. Boys covered with paint or grease threatened to smear themselves on passersby unless they donated a small coin. Change in hand, we enjoyed the costumes and marching bands but mostly stuck to our errands and went to bed early. For much of cruising's hard work occurs in ports, figuring things out and tramping from place to place.

Always seeking alternatives to the upwind slog, we looked for transport to the Putumayo River, which flows into the Amazon, but it was too far away, on the Ecuadorian border where guerrilla warfare persisted. Then we noticed that Puerto Cabello, Venezuela, is only seventy miles from a tributary of the Rio Apure, which flows into the Orinoco. If we could get to the confluence of the Apure and the Orinoco we could either turn left, coming out the mouth of the Orinoco as I did in 1991, or right, ascending the Orinoco. In the latter case we could take the Brazo Casiquiare to the Rio Negro, thence to the Amazon.

With carnival performer in Cartagena, Colombia.
I am wielding the stick we accidentally stole from the junkman.

Don Starkell, author of *Paddle to the Amazon,* used the Casiquiare in 1981. It is one of few places in the world where one can navigate up one river system and down another without portaging, due to a freak connection in their respective headwaters. Puerto Cabello was still 750 nautical miles away, but it was a lot closer than Trinidad. From Trinidad we could turn left and return to the States via the greater and lesser Antilles. Going up the Orinoco we would probably still end up in Trinidad eventually, after a major excursion into South America.

Paperwork was a worry. Colombia required that boat captains engage a shipping agent whenever entering an official port. The regulation was meant for large vessels, but was enforced on yachts as well. The agent charged a substantial fee for obtaining entry and clearance documents. Consequently we decided to bypass the two remaining Colombian ports, Barranquilla and Santa Marta. What's more, Venezuela had no port of entry until Puerto Cabello, so we got a clearance for that city though it would take us weeks to get there. In the meantime we would have legally left Colombia and not yet have legally entered Venezuela. Wherever we went ashore we could be violating the immigration laws of one country or the other. Laws like this are so mean-spirited! They force poor seafarers to commit victimless crimes. That illegality can then be used by corrupt officials to obtain bribes.

We left on November 12th. The trade winds soon kicked in so we rarely sailed anymore. We motored past the gargantuan, hyacinth-choked mouth of the Rio Magdalena to a small town south of Santa Marta. Here we got out and pulled the boat by hand into a knee-deep stream. A big rain had just passed, so the current was swift. We had pulled *Thurston* a hundred yards up the right bank when suddenly the water level shot up and roller-coaster waves formed in the middle of the stream! We dug our anchors into the bank to avoid being swept away in the flash flood. The waves reared up tall and closely spaced, debris floating by at eye-blink speed. Suddenly the waves collapsed into a roaring brown foam. Then they grew again, and collapsed again. The process repeated itself over and over: waves growing to five feet in height, collapsing, and reforming. This furious rhythm slowly died during the night until cricket chirps could again be heard. In the morning the flood was spent. Egrets fished at the stream mouth. *Thurston* lay high and dry on the sand. Some fishermen helped us push her back into the water.

Flash flood near Santa Marta, Colombia

After Santa Marta the winds became stronger, the waves bigger. Even at full throttle, masts down to reduce windage, a square-on wave collision would often bring us to a standstill. First our bow would fly up, then it would fall while our stern lifted, causing the propellor to rev in mid-air. To counteract this we stopped in a semi-protected lagoon, brought the motor ashore, and made a lower mounting plate. The area was a national park. A ten-minute walk through mangrove and dark forest brought us to an eco-tourism center, where someone with an electric drill punched the holes for the new plate. With the motor four inches lower the cavitations largely stopped. This allowed us to continue rounding the bulge caused by the Sierra Nevada de Santa Marta, a mountain range rising abruptly to 18,700 feet above sea level. It's the only place where snow is visible from the Caribbean Sea. The mountains were so tall and close we had to crane our necks. They faded into mist in the sky to our right. Occasionally we saw whiteness up there, but it may have been the sun reflecting on bare rock. The mountain range protruded into the sea with many headlands and steep-to bays, giving us safe places to stop for the night.

*At Parque Nacional Tayrona in the Sierra Nevada de Santa Marta.
The previous day we sailed past the breakers visible in the background,
found a pass, and doubled back inside the lagoon to work on the boat
and sleep. Now we are taking the Honda back to the boat.*

The same could not be said for the following stretch of coast, at
the base of the Guajira Peninsula. After a hard day of twenty-knot
headwinds we investigated a river mouth to see if we could enter it.
While motoring back and forth studying the breakers I strayed too
close. A rogue wave broke over the motor, drowning it! We quickly
threw out the anchor, but in the minute it took for it to catch, and
with the subsequent pay-out of line, *Thurston* drifted further in. The
swells here were breaking! The cockpit filled repeatedly. The motor
wouldn't start. We risked total loss.

I threw on my swimsuit, fins, mask and snorkel. Unsure whether
Ginny could make it through the surf I left her aboard while I swam to
shore, maybe two hundred yards away. Then I ran along the beach to
the river mouth. Inside the water was calm and shallow enough to
wade. On the other side, where a dirt road led into the town of Dibulla,

fishermen were tending their nets and motors. Descending on them like an apparition I offered fifteen dollars to whoever would tow *Thurston* in. One agreed. He gathered up gas and crew while I anxiously peered seaward. *Thurston* and my wife were invisible much of the time, hidden in wave troughs. Meanwhile Ginny held on tight but was prepared to abandon ship. The swells were breaking over the boat. Some of them caught *Thurston* on her side, tipping the low gunwale underwater, threatening capsize.

Finally the skipper motored to *Thurston*. The operation required skill. First we got under *Thurston's* anchor line and pulled the anchor aboard. Then we towed *Thurston* with the line. *"Eso es muy peligroso"* (This is very dangerous), the skipper mumbled, perhaps regretting he'd accepted my offer. Coming into the mouth both boats yawed violently but the skipper kept up a good speed. *Thurston* was soon safe on the tranquil river. I gave him more money than I had mentioned, and thanked him profusely. Now that the drama had passed we settled into our evening routine. The sun set, the wind died. The motor started once I'd cleared the water out of the air intake and carburetor.

As we traveled northeast around the Guajira Peninsula the dominant plant became a tall, scraggly cactus. Walking ashore I flushed what appeared to be a green bird with dangling red tail feathers. It re-landed a short distance away. I looked closer. It wasn't a bird at all! It was a huge grasshopper with red legs! We saw Guajiro Indians in stick-and-mud houses and wooden fishing smacks. They were quiet and undemonstrative. As we proceeded northeast, low beaches gave way to orange-tan cliffs. Wrecked ships dotted the bluff coasts. Boats couldn't land there so nobody lived there.

Our final night in Colombia we spent in Puerto Estrella, a bay sufficiently protected from the northeast swell to anchor safely but not comfortably. Following local practice we anchored *Thurston* bow-on to the swells and ran a stern line to a dead tree. Boys swam out and climbed aboard without asking. We shooed them off. Swimming ashore we found a desert hamlet at the end of a dirt road leading into the interior. We bought gas from a woman who sold it in soft-drink containers from her house.

Sleeping moored like that is unforgettable. A steep surge causes a sharp jerking forward and backward. When the stern line comes taut the boat stops and you jerk forward, like you were underway and you've hit something. Then the bow line comes taut and you jerk backward. Repeat that like a metronome all night. The best defense is to lay flat on your back on the boat's centerline. We never discovered a way to accommodate it psychologically, allowing us to sleep. This was unfortunate because our next leg was a long crossing to Los Monjes, an archipelago belonging to the Venezuelan navy.

On November 21, 2011, we motored northeast from Colombia's Guajira Peninsula. Twenty-five miles out we found Los Monjes, a scattering of rock pinnacles. The largest two stand side-by-side. To create a base the Venezuelan Navy had leveled some building pads and dumped the spoils between the two islands until they were connected by a causeway. We tied to a mooring rope. They searched *Thurston,* chiding us for not carrying various items for which we had no room. They even wanted to know if we had semaphore flags, which went out of fashion around World War I! Once they released us we were free to hike and swim, but the place seemed claustrophobic. The barracks were full of bored sailors.

Again the headwind decreased at night so we left in the predawn for the Paraguana Peninsula, forty-eight miles away. The two peninsulas, Guajira and Paraguana, were our principle obstacles on the way to Puerto Cabello. No land was visible until a faint blue mountain stood out, then low hills. In the afternoon we located Punta Macolla, where a half-dozen wooden boats huddled behind a small point, jostling in the swells. On the beach was a crude fishing camp. Beyond stretched flat desert.

To get around this second cape we left at 3:00 a.m. This time our luck ran out. An hour into the passage the east wind picked up until salt spray blinded us. The motor wasn't powerful enough to keep her head to the seas, so *Thurston's* bow kept turning one way or the other. We cowered over the compass, bracing against the belly-flops, hoping to break through to the other side of the storm. The Honda 2HP only has a one-liter internal tank; it can't be fed by a hose. When the tank ran dry I refilled it, a hard job in the best of conditions because the motor was suspended aft of *Thurston's* stern. I had to balance myself precariously and handle more objects than I had hands for. In the process water must have entered the tank because when I pulled the starter cord nothing happened. We deployed the sea anchor to control drift while troubleshooting the engine. Nothing worked. We needed to sail back to Punta Macolla, but could we raise the masts in those waves? If not we would end up back at the Monjes. Summoning our courage, I lifted the masts while Ginny wrestled their bases into their steps. After a few failed attempts we got them both in. Then we unfurled a bit of sail, and by sunrise we were back at the fishing camp.

I unbolted the motor and carried it to a plywood shack with a table made from a defunct refrigerator. The fishermen, swarthy men in their thirties and forties, drained the carburetor and changed the gas in the tank. They soon had it running like new, no charge. They advised us to wait a few days before attempting the cape again, so we decided to sail south into the Gulf of Venezuela, where there are towns and protective bays.

Ever since Panama cruisers we met had been warning us not to go to Venezuela due to rampant crime and governmental hostility. "Prepare to be robbed every day!" one friendly man warned. For us Venezuela was the lesser of several evils so we had continued, always fearful that the next boat that passed would be pirates. But once again everyone seemed friendly.

We sailed thirty miles south to a small city called Punto Fijo. Here we were directed to the *Club Nautico*, a yacht club with a dock and dry storage. We moored there among several tall sport-fishing boats. A pair of naval officers stepped down into *Thurston* to commence another search. The water was calm as a mill pond until the wake from a passing vessel generated a series of vertical waves. These slammed *Thurston* repeatedly against a steel piling with a crunching sound! The naval officers, caught unaware, scrambled out ot *Thurston* and fled. Search over!

We couldn't bring ourselves to look at the damage just then. We anchored just offshore, bow to waves, stern to beach. She was safe now but jerked violently with each surge, like in Puerto Estrella. A weekend-long fishing tournament was getting underway. More boats arrived. Excited crews prepped their engines and hauled beer aboard. Merry-makers thronged the beach at the base of the dock. Electronic Latin rap music blasted from multiple sources. We were depressed and uncomfortable. When the tournament ended we examined *Thurston*.

The port gunwale was badly broken at the leeboard pivot and the side deck had a split two feet long.

Damage from smashing against a piling during inspection, Punto Fijo

Fortunately the club members helped us. They hauled *Thurston* out, set her on a concrete slab, and gave us a power yacht to live in while we repaired the damage. After weeks of sun, salt, and motion we thrived on the comfort. We had a hose, a power outlet, and a shower stall in an otherwise broken back bathroom. The Venezuelans, respectful of our nautical spirit, were eager to lend a hand or a tool. A shopping mall was 25 minutes away by foot. We bought Venezuelan *bolívares* at a downtown store that doubled as a currency black market. The economy seemed to be a boisterous free market weighted down by an egalitarian but inefficient layer of socialism. The Club Nautico members were not big fans of Hugo Chavez.

The repairs took ten days. We rolled *Thurston* over, gouged out disintegrated fiberglass, applied new glass and epoxy in a series of lay-ups, and replaced broken wooden parts. We restored her integrity and reduced her scars to an acceptable level. The slimy authorities charged us $270 for permission to sail to Puerto Cabello. That was by far the largest entry fee we'd paid so far, but the *Club Nautico* charged us nothing, so we came out okay.

It was time to tackle the Paraguana peninsula again. We had used up all our epoxy resin, so we resolved to stop off at Aruba along the way because that island had a marine supply store. One of the Dutch Antilles, Aruba lay an extra twenty miles north of the cape. The wind was so strong we got down to six reefs in the main and four in the mizzen, which is about as reefed as *Thurston* got, but finally we reached Aruba, where we hid in some mangrove. To avoid paying Venezuelan entry fees again we didn't clear in. Beyond the mangroves was a dry landscape dominated by cactus and palm trees. We walked to the boating goods store, then took a bus downtown to get U.S. cash for use in Venezuela. Two cruise ships were in port. Tourists crowded the jewelry stores and casinos. The multi-ethnic people spoke English, Spanish, and Dutch, but mostly Papimiento, a mixture of all the above.

At 2:00 a.m. on our second night in Aruba, while we were anchored in a cove at the southeast tip, an Aruban coast guard boat pulled alongside. "Why haven't you passed Immigration?" they asked.

"We're not going on land," I prevaricated. "We're just anchoring here, on our way to Venezuela. We're leaving early in the morning." That part was true.

"I'm afraid you're going to have to come with us back to town," they said. Then they noticed that a stray line had gotten wrapped around their propeller. They couldn't get it free. I put on my trunks and mask, dove in, and sawed through it with a knife. Happy to be set free, they returned the favor by departing without us.

The following day, as we finally rounded the troublesome Paraguana Peninsula, I performed the following song which I had made up for Ginny's benefit. The tune is obvious.

> Venezuela here we come, right back where we started from!
> You're friendly, but deadly, we like it that way!
> Charged us too much money but we're gonna stay, I tell ya
> Venezuela here we come, 'cuz Aruba can't be done
> We are sailing into the sun
> Venezuela here we come!

Ginny showed no pleasure in this ditty, but she was sorely glad to reach Adicora, a town with lovely old Spanish-Dutch buildings and, most importantly, calm water thanks to a protective reef.

We next sailed to La Vela, at the eastern base of the peninsula. Since leaving Punto Fijo we had mostly sailed because our course was northeast, then southeast. These directions are sailable when the wind is from the east. From La Vela, however, we had to motor straight into the easterlies again. Starting in the predawn we droned through long days. The coast was endless, empty of people, covered with low shrubbery, green because the rainy season wasn't over yet. At Chichiriviche we angled southeast across open sea to cross the Gulfo Triste.

On December 14 we entered Puerto Cabello, our goal for so long. Since leaving Bocas del Toro we had traveled 1,500 nautical miles, far more per day than in previous phases. It was into the wind but we had the motor. We had learned to avoid winds over twenty knots and waves capable of drowning the motor. Within these constraints, the motorized Sea Pearl is reliable and efficient: we had used only eighteen gallons of gas.

The only place we were allowed to stay was the municipal marina. The manager was aghast when she saw that the officials in Punto Fijo had not given us a *permiso de estadia,* or cruising permit. "You could be arrested, your boat confiscated!" she exclaimed. She urged us to leave immediately for Curaçao, a Dutch island a hundred miles north, then sail to Puerto La Cruz, far to the east, and clear back in there, because only those officials were authorized to issue cruising permits. Then we could backtrack to Puerto Cabello. This scenario would mean traveling an extra 550 miles, with impossibly long passages, at the wrong time of year, risking our lives because someone to whom we paid $270 had failed to give us the right paper! A customs agent said that something might be worked out in Puerto Cabello but it would take months and be *very* expensive.

Dazed, we sat in a covered seating area where the local sport fishermen socialized. A birthday party for one of them was just starting. They fired up a barbecue and filled coolers with ice and Polar beer. When they realized who we were they showered us with drinks and food. As in Punto Fijo the generosity of the people ameliorated the greed and incompetence of the government. One of the attendees, an employee at the Port Captain's office, promised to help us get the cruising permit.

In the meantime we were stuck in a hellacious marina. The breakwater only partly blocked the swell, so boats and floating docks surged violently. Vessels broke loose, became battering rams. We fixed the breakage and bought heavier docking lines. When the ramp leading from our floating dock up to the breakwater broke off a fellow boater tied an old dinghy in place as a makeshift bridge.

Getting ashore using an inflatable as a floating bridge,
Puerto Cabello Marina, Venezuela.

The water was polluted with spilled gasoline and oil. Dogs and seabirds sifted through mounds of garbage stockpiled along the breakwater. The water system was out of order. The restrooms were unspeakable; people just defecated on top of the excrement already piled up there. All this municipal incompetence jarred with billboards all over the city wherein the mayor touted his many fine achievements, with fetching smiles and dynamic gestures. "Socialism is efficient!" proclaimed one. Like President Hugo Chavez he always wore a red shirt. Another showed them standing together, arms around each other's shoulders.

Puerto Cabello seemed to be shredded into different time periods. We were in the historic port district where the buildings were tall and graceful with finely molded facades, but dilapidated, often in total ruin. Further away the buildings were squat and common-wall. Residents commonly sat on the curb in front of their homes or in one of the little plazas with a statue in the center. There were no drains, so even mild rains spread puddles across the streets. The modern architecture along the highway was relatively deserted.

Out-of-town Venezuelans thronged the downtown public waterfront during the Christmas holidays. For three weeks music blasted from food-and-drink stalls on the beach on one side of us and from a carnival strip on the other. We had only to exit the marina gates to peruse the rides and games of skill and chance. Endless beer was consumed, much of it around a liquor store where they sold cups through a barred window. Venezuelans often didn't finish their last inch or so beer, giving rise to the "beer bum" phenomenon. When a patron reached that last inch the bum held out his mug and the patron poured it over. On weekend afternoons the beer bums were cheerful indeed! We were grateful for the security post that kept the masses out of the marina.

The laptop broke so we ordered a new one from the States. At internet places we Facebooked and word-processed. New Years Eve came and went. We got dental work done. Three times we traveled to Valencia, the nearest big city, to see the movie "Tin Tin," but it was always sold out or cancelled. Much of cruising is simply doing familiar things in unfamiliar circumstances, therefore inefficiently and with endless frustration! With the frugality that comes from living on savings we walked a lot and compared prices. Just figuring out the phone system of each new country was daunting. Avoiding ATMs we took our dollars to a men's clothing shop where we illegally got twice as many *bolivares* as we could at a bank. When we ran out of cash dollars we used PayPal to transfer funds to the U.S. bank account of an affluent Venezuelan. Once it cleared he gave us the correct amount in *bolivares*. We jumped through these hoops to circumvent the rigged government rate. The dollar prices we quote here are based on the black market rate, which represents how much people outside the country are willing to pay for *bolivares*.

Our Honda two-horse now emitted a horrible screech whenever we started it up, so we took it to a mechanic. He allowed us to watch while he disassembled the lower unit, pulled out the vertical shaft, and removed the engine. The motor had an automatic centrifugal clutch, the ball bearing of which had rusted solid. Saltwater had reached it. Fortunately it was a standard part, easily replaced.

Mechanic fixing motor, Puerto Cabello, Venezuela

After three weeks of intermittent groveling at the *capitania* and another $220 contribution to the government (or to corrupt officials, one never knows which) we got our cruising permit. While waiting I had gone by bus to a town called El Baul and determined that the Rio Cojedes was navigable. We knew from scrutinizing Google Earth at internet cafes that it flows into the Portuguese, which flows into the Apure, which flows into the Orinoco. When we reached the Orinoco we would decide whether to turn left, back to the ocean, or right, to the Amazon.

Chapter 5
UP THE ORINOCO, DOWN THE NEGRO

We found a transporter willing to haul us to the river system for $330. On January 13, 2012, he pulled us out onto a trailer. We rode with him as he towed *Thurston* over coastal hills then down into the Llanos (pronounced yawn-ose), the great plains of northern South America, showing his permits at the many police and military check-points. We were bumping along a deteriorated stretch of roadway when we saw up ahead three teenagers sitting in the road with shovels. When they noticed us coming they sprang up and started tossing gravel into a pothole. As we slowed down to pass they dropped their tools and ran alongside with a jar, banging and yelling for tips. Our driver ignored them. Crestfallen, they fell behind to wait for their next "customer."

At the town of El Baul we backed the trailer into a brown stream about twenty-five feet wide. With a quick *"Adios!"* we pushed off into the moderate current. The banks were tall and thick with willows. Beyond were forests and farms with cattle, pigs, and chickens. When it got dark we tied to a branch. The evening was cool. A praying mantis alighted on the tiller, facing forward, his little hands at chest height. Then he rocked sideways back and forth like a metronome. The eyes of a nearby alligator reflected red in our headlamps.

On the second day the Rio Cojedes joined the larger Rio Portuguese. On the fourth day the latter joined the far larger Apure. All flowed southeast gathering frequent tributaries. Their "meander factor" (river distance divided by straight-line distance) was a hefty 1.6. Each day we started rowing at six or seven. After a couple hours the

Launching in the Rio Cojedes, Venezuela

east wind got too strong so we motored at low throttle, appreciating the assist from the current. We averaged seventy kilometers per day.

Howler monkeys picked fruits in the tall trees. Smaller monkeys sipped from the river and retreated into the foliage on our approach. The trees and brush were thronged with a bird that resembles a chicken or a pheasant except that it has a Mohawk crest and its call is similar to that of a crow. (We learned later that it's called the hoatzin.) There were kingfishers, pink flamingos, cormorants, roseate spoonbills, cranes, scarlet macaws, emerald parakeets, and, yes! pink dolphins.

I was used to them from my earlier voyage, but not Ginny. They were blue-grey on top blending to pink on bottom, with bulbous foreheads. Sometimes they breached just long enough for a quick breath, other times they splashed their tails or leapt clear of the water. Whenever we rowed or motored at low speed as many as ten dolphins followed us, sometimes ahead, sometimes behind.

The houses on the banks were generally simple, the people dark and slender. They stared as we passed. The men wore cowboy hats or

96

River dolphin following us, Venezuela

baseball caps. Some emitted a high yelp that serves as their jocular greeting. Their boats were steel canoes with square transoms and long, overhanging bows for transferring people and goods onto steep banks. They ran with their motors wide open, usually a forty-horse Yamaha two-stroke. In the towns people rode mules, horses, and Chinese motorcycles.

After three days on the Apure we reached San Fernando, capital of the state of Apure. Under a tall bridge men shoveled sand from steel canoes into trucks. Further down thirty or forty boats were parked gunwale-to-gunwale, bows onto a steep beach covered with stranded water hyacinth. We landed among much hubbub and explored this metropolis of the plains.

We worked at an internet shop, had a new sail cover made, and bought batteries. A historian told of us Simon Bolivar´s travails in Apure during the wars of independence. At a government bookstore, where books boosting revolutionary awareness were heavily subsidized, I bought several novels. A poet I met there said he could get the

San Fernando de Apure, Venezuela

government to publish my writings if I translated them into Spanish! I doubted whether my observations would get through the censor. I also took advantage of the subsidized gasoline. Catching a motor-cycle-taxi to a gas station I bought six gallons for the equivalent of $0.04 per gallon! No wonder the Venezuelan boats always ran with their motors wide open.

On January 21 mountains became visible to the southeast. A gap opened, then the Rio Apure, which had seemed huge, emptied into the Orinoco. It was several kilometers wide counting the islands. Its blue-brown surface surged with upswells. The land was drier now. The summer had started and vast areas of beach were exposed, like deserts with blowing sand.

We needed to stay close to civilization until a package arrived so we went down the Orinoco to Caicara, a dull town on the south bank. For security we arranged to stay at the naval base, tying up next to their boat. I'd spent three weeks in Caicara in 1992. This was the first time we visited a place familiar to me from my earlier voyage. I was unable to locate my ne'er-do-well friend, El Maraycucho, nor the sidewalk café I was sitting in when the radio announced that Air Force colonel Hugo Chavez and co-conspirators had bombed the presidential palace in a coup attempt. (He failed and went to prison, yet was subsequently elected president.) The view from the river bluff was unchanged, however: a horizon-to-horizon expanse of white-capped bronze water and barren sand flats.

To pick up our package and get visas for Brazil we took a bus to Caracas, the capital. Caracas had the highest homicide rate in the world, so we planned meticulously for the trip. The bus left in the afternoon and deposited us the following dawn in a three-story downtown bus station. We spent the day in crowded subways and walking apprehensively among skyscrapers. The package was waiting for us at a suburban office, but the official at the Brazilian embassy said it would take five days to process our visas. This was harsh news. Yet he was compassionate. He heard us out while we described how the Venezuelan government had been treating us. Pretty soon he launched into his own anti-Venezuelan rant; serving at this post had irritated him to no end. "I agree, they're absolutely impossible," he concluded. "You know what, I'll see what I can do." At four p.m. the visas were done! It pays to enlist mutual antipathies.

Having accomplished our goals in a single day we caught a bus back to Caicara that same night. Back aboard, we caught up on sleep and enthused over our package. Ginny's mom had shipped the new laptop, hatch covers, motor parts, and pressure cooker parts as requested, and had thrown in some treats for good measure!

Thurston was working great as a river boat, so we'd decided to go up the Orinoco to the Brazo Casiquiare, which joins with the Negro, a major tributary of the Amazon. There were no maps, so we went to an internet place, turned on Google Earth, and clicked with the mouse to trace the shorelines, islands, shoals, tributary mouths, and towns. Ginny converted the tracks to Garmin files and loaded them onto our GPSmap 60CSx. In effect we made our own electronic chart of the rivers to Brazil. Most importantly, we wanted it to tell us whether to go left or right whenever we hit a shoal. One shortcoming was that the satellite photos were sometimes years old, and the rivers may have changed course. Another was that they were generally taken at a different time of year, when the water could be up to forty feet higher or lower than currently. In the event, the islands had shifted considerably since the date of the imagery, but our map was sufficient.

From El Baul to Caicara the current had been in our favor while the wind was against us. This was reversed as we sailed upriver toward Puerto Ayacucho. The same trade winds we had fought on the coast now favored us. Our speed through the water averaged ten kilometers per hour, but the current was three kph for a net speed of seven kph. The GPS helped us find secluded beaches at which to stop for the night. They had to be on the north or east side of the river to avoid the waves kicked up by the northeast wind, and there couldn't be any houses nearby. If no boats passed by until full darkness, and if we shone no lights, no one would become aware of us. Unfortunately, at dusk fishermen came out to set their nets and bait their hooks. Whenever they saw us we had to move. They were honest and hardworking, but we were very strange to them, and they might mention our presence to predatory people.

One night we thought we had the perfect place, inside a calm cove in the sand flats. But as we waded ashore, pulling *Thurston* over high spots in the sandy bottom, a powerboat approached. They stopped at a shoal, barely visible in the gathering gloom. Two men got out and splashed toward us yelling something.

"What is he yelling?" I asked Ginny.

"It sounds like, "*Hombre!*"" We kept pulling.

Suddenly I realized the word was *nombre,* a demand that we identify ourselves. I faced the men, now twenty yards away. One racked the action of a rifle and aimed it at me. "*Manos arriba! Nombre!*" I raised my hands and answered, "*Turistas!*"

It turned out we had passed a turtle nursery protected by a *Guardia Nacional* post and they thought we were turtle poachers! We followed them across the river and slept next to their facility. In the morning they showed us three tanks full of baby Arrau tortoises, one of several species that used to be common. When we held them in our hands they folded their heads and tails sideways into their shells. Not only were they saving the turtles, they gave us free watermelon, so we forgave them for threatening to shoot us.

On February 6 we reached the Rio Meta, an east-west river that joins the Orinoco at a right angle. The north bank of the Meta is Venezuela, the south bank is Colombia. We stopped at Puerto Carreño, on the Colombian side. Colombia and Venezuela used to be one country so it is interesting to compare their progress. Colombia has been plagued by guerrillas and drug lords while Venezuela is rolling in oil, so you would think that the latter would be more advanced. But after ten weeks in Venezuela, this bit of Colombia looked cleaner, wealthier, and less militarized. We felt free here! Colombian tourists could be seen taking pictures from the local hilltop and drinking beer at an outdoor bar. We got money from an ATM, checked into Colombia so as to restart our ninety-day clock upon re-entry in Venezuela, and left for Puerto Ayacucho.

The Portuguese and Apure rivers had flowed through flat *llanos*. On the Orinoco we still had the *llanos* to starboard but to port lay the Guyana Massif, consisting of blue hills and rounded, glossy-grey rocks of volcanic origin. Sometimes these rocks were emergent from the earth, other times they were mounded boulders the size of cars or

Round rocks, Upper Orinoco

houses. Many were split. They were smooth but roughly textured. They often lay partly submerged in the tan sand. Trees, rocks, sand, water, sky, and fluffy clouds combined nicely in the landscape. We climbed among the boulders for views, and hiked across tracts of cracked mud. The flats were often thick with a stalky bush that bends easily when underwater but stands upright when the waters recede.

A day and a half above Puerto Carreño we reached Puerto Ayacucho, capital of the Venezuelan state of Amazonas, a road-less area stretching south and east to Brazil. Above Puerto Ayacucho there are impassible rapids, but the river is navigable again starting at a place called Samariapo. We stopped at a *Guardia Nacional* post where a lieutenant gave *Thurston* her harshest search to date. He kept lambasting us for one imaginary equipment deficiency after another. We sat passively until he left in frustration, whereupon a bystander commended us for not having given him a bribe. They don't demand money, rather they intimidate you until you volunteer it. But they are less self-assured with tourists. We could ignore this guy whereas a Venezuelan would have paid.

We next proceeded to the only viable access to town: the naval base. Here the sailors belabored us for hours with questions, instructions, and precautions. We then climbed three flights of steps through an open docking structure designed to accommodate boats both in the dry season and in the rainy season, when the river rises. Passing through the compound's gates we entered the city and began our quest for permits and another portage.

Here I offer up a homey detail that will put the reader right there with us. The day is over and our traipsing about town is done. The awning is up. I recline in "the throne," our word for the most comfortable place to sit. Its seat is the cockpit floor softened by a cushion. My back is against the lazarette, the forward surface of which I had designed to provide lower back support when so seated. My arms are on the cockpit seats which in this position are at elbow height. My feet are up on the bridge deck just aft of the companionway (the entry into the cabin). I have just eaten another delicious dinner concocted under difficult circumstances by Ginny. She, resting from her labors, lays in bed, head on pillows, heels propped up on the companionway ledge. I paste my toothbrush and put it in my mouth. Then I paste Ginny's brush and stick it between two of my toes. I then extend that foot, wiggle the toothbrush from my toes into her toes, and say, "Toe-jam telegram!" She is now obliged to clean her teeth. Otherwise she might not get around to it.

Our first stop in Puerto Ayacucho was the immigration station, where we got stamped back into Venezuela. On our way back we saw a sign saying Tourist Information. Upon our knock a white-haired gentleman opened the door.

"Good day, Virgilio Limpias, at your service. How can I help you?" Virgilio was born in Bolivia. After studying medicine he came to the Amazonas to work with the natives. He ended up marrying a local and starting a guide service while running a small medical practice. When we told him our plan his perpetual grin grew even wider, his mannerisms more animated. "Thirty years I've guided people into the Amazonas, and in all that time only two other parties have gone through in their own boats!"

"What do you remember about them?"

"One was a French couple. The other was a father-and-son team, I don't remember their nationality." The latter must have been Don and Dana Starkell of *Paddle to the Amazon*. The time frame was correct. He showed us the maps he had gathered and the tour guide he had written. He confided to us his own dream, which was to someday follow rivers all the way to Montevideo, Uruguay. We took note of the river route he mentioned.

"The permits will be difficult," he warned.

"Do you have a boat trailer?" I asked.

"Oh yes, no problem."

I hired him, the compensation to be decided later. During the coming week Virgilio's extroversion, patience, energy, and humor opened doors for us. He knew most of the officials and in many cases had doctored their families. We obtained a customs dispatch, a post-dated passport exit stamp (because there is no immigration office on the Brazilian border), a port captain clearance, a road permit to move the boat, a permit from the state petroleum company to buy a hundred liters of fuel, a fuel-tracking document from the *Guardia Nacional* (to be validated at military posts along the way to prove that we were not reselling the fuel to Colombians or Brazilians), and a permit from the bureau governing the indigenous people. The latter was the most difficult because 52nd Army Brigadier General Jesus Manuel Zambrano Mata himself had to sign it!

We were questioned by a captain in the Military Intelligence Department of the 52nd Army Brigade, also by a major in Military Counter-Intelligence. They opposed letting unescorted foreigners into the area. A colonel pulled Virgilio aside. "The next world war is going to be for water!" he intoned. "The Yankees want to conquer our Amazonas watershed! These people may be spies."

"Nonsense! With their satellites the Americans can count the fillings in your teeth! They don't need spies!"

"But they may be here to collect water samples!" he protested. Virgilio laughed it off, but confided to us his hatred for President Hugo Chavez and his military bullies.

Some uniformed personnel were nice. In the evenings we sat with the sailors in their lounge. We worked on our laptops, connected to their power and wi-fi, while they watched "Rocky" or "Rambo" videos translated into Spanish. Others looked for any irregularity in our papers to denounce us. Our nationality was a handicap. Chavez was rabidly anti-Yankee. He even accused the United States of giving him and other South American presidents cancer by means of a new satellite technology!

Transparency International was giving Venezuela the worst corruption rating in Latin America. Crime had driven the tourists away. The government was appropriating land and businesses without compensation. Inflation was running at 30% annually. A newspaper article described how eighty-four people had died in a mafia war for control of union jobs in the state petroleum corporation! Chavez had already been president for thirteen years, but he was running yet again. His party used government funds to place its messages on government vehicles, uniforms, and billboards. His image was everywhere. We concealed our disgust.

The Navy, National Guard, and National Institute of Aquatic Spaces all searched *Thurston*. The grand finale was an especially meticulous tear-down by Military Intelligence. It took seven men three hours to remove and examine everything. They even checked our camera and computer storage devices for incriminating material! They found quite interesting our copy of the Small Craft Advisor magazine in which our article about Cuba appeared, because Cuba was their ally. During the process the ranking officer sidled up to me and whispered into my ear, "I want to go to America!" Like this was the Cold War and he wanted to defect to the West! I just chuckled and waited.

On February 17, 2012, Virgilio loaded *Thurston* onto a trailer and towed us with his Toyota pickup over a paved road to Samariapo, a landing upstream of the rapids. About a hundred boats were there, mostly *bongos* (long, slender, steel canoes with outboard motors) transporting people and supplies up the river. I gave Virgilio the equivalent of about $600 for the permits and portage, and a hug. "Virgilio, you have earned your money!"

Virgilio Limpias schmoozing the soldiers at Samariapo

As we continued upstream Venezuela was still on our left, Colombia on our right. The border region was tense because the armed forces of the two countries were hostile toward each other; Colombian *guerrilleros* sometimes took refuge on the Venezuelan side. And the current grew stronger. If it flowed too fast in one channel we found another. The worst was a cataract strewn with huge boulders. We would come to a stop then drift left or right seeking a slower riffle. We carried a long, strong tow rope in case we had to seek a tow through a rapid, but we always managed to inch our way through. There were now hills on both sides. The forest was denser. At the town of San Fernando de Atabapo the river turned southeast. Both banks were now Venezuelan.

The river shrank as we passed tributary mouths. Running our motor at two-thirds throttle we skirted sandbars and globular granite rocks. Our hundred liters of fuel resided in twenty-liter containers lashed to either side of the cabin. As they emptied we gave them away. We used up the last of our bread and fruit and dug into the canned food.

Each day we passed an indigenous community or two. They typically consisted of ten or so neat mud-and-wattle houses and an assembly hall around a grassy commons. North American missionaries had established these settlements but Chavez had subsequently expelled them. In some villages the natives spoke Wotuja, in others Kurripako, not that we could tell the difference. They mostly ate fish, yucca, and plantains. They were friendly and quiet. We stopped at *Guardia Nacional* checkpoints and got our papers stamped. The soldiers were bored and listless.

All day we droned upriver with our earplugs in, probing with our boat hook to check water depth, skirting sandbars. We now passed *tepuys*: huge mesas such as Sir Arthur Conan Doyle popularized in his book *The Lost World*. Scarlet macaws flew overhead in twos and threes cawing like crows. Large black-and-yellow birds tended their young in teardrop-shaped nests hanging from the trees; we had first seen them in Monkey Bay, Nicaragua. Rust-breasted kingfishers flew from one overlooking branch to another. Then Jackpot! Ginny spotted an animal swimming across the river. I motored over. It was a giant anteater! It reached the far bank and pulled itself out of the water. We gasped as it revealed its full length, perhaps seven feet counting its long, droopy snout and big bushy tail!

On our seventh day out of Puerto Ayacucho we reached the geographic phenomenon we had long yearned for: the Brazo Casiquiare!

Giant ant eater, Orinoco River

There was no signpost, no break in the uninterrupted jungle. Maybe one tenth of the Orinoco simply split off and disappeared south toward the Amazon. We had reached the hump! Up to this point a mechanical malfunction could have forced us back down the Orinoco. Now the current would help us explore a new basin.

At first the Casiquiare was about fifty yards wide and the same turbid brown color as the Orinoco. It quickly widened as tributaries joined in. These, flowing from local swamps, were translucent black. As a consequence the Casiquiare gradually became blacker and clearer. We didn't want to rush, but the immigration officials in Puerto Ayacucho had given us very little time on our exit stamp, which they postdated because there would be no other immigration post on our route. So we fell into a new pattern of rowing three hours per day and motoring for six. Our maps showed communities but they didn't exist. For four days, averaging seventy kilometers per day, we saw no sign of man on shore and only a couple boats on the water. Often one of us steered while the other played the guitar, sewed, read, or washed clothes.

Split rock, Brazo Casiquiare, Venezuela

We camped at scenic confluences or next to dramatic rocks. In the twilight bats fluttered about. It was frustrating to hear strange night calls and not know what was making them: birds, bats, insects, monkeys? By day a new species of biting insect plagued us, between a mosquito and a no-see-um in size. Its itchy bites left a red dot in the center of a pink blotch. We battled one ant invasion after another and learned to tie up to trees standing in water so they couldn't come aboard. One morning a coral snake slowly swam along the swampy shore we were tied to. "Red next to yellow you're a dead fellow, red next to black you're alright Jack," recited Ginny. "He's got red next to yellow so he's poisonous!" But our most significant wildlife sighting was a cougar. Despite decades of adventuring in the Pacific Northwest I had never seen one, and here we surprised one swimming across the river! In this situation large mammals are very aware of their vulnerability. I was steering. We saw each other at the same time. His head was round and tan with small ears. He was a quarter of the way across, swimming from left to right. Realizing we would intercept him

108

in the middle he immediately turned around and swam back with amazing speed. He stared at us until we passed.

Back at the turtle sanctuary on the Orinoco River we had seen a map showing a related refuge on the Casiquiare, and had noted its location. Sure enough, we found a place where boats landed. On the bank were a rough shelter and three or four big tubs with young turtles in them. Most looked to be dead or dying. No one was around. There was no sign, no explanation.

On the fifth day we stopped at a Yanomami settlement. They are usually photographed wearing loincloths with narrow sticks inserted horizontally through the flesh of their faces, but these people wore factory-made shorts and skirts. Ginny swam in the river with a crowd of happy children while a young man under five feet in height showed me around the village. He showed me his thatched hut, in which he had a bow, beautiful arrows longer than he was tall, and a CD player. On the way back we stopped at an open shelter where a handsome boy was hypnotically chanting and dancing on the hard-packed earth. He wore paint on his face and arms. Short feather arrays projected from either side of his head. My Spanish-speaking guide said he was under the influence of a drug, a powder that one person blows into the nostrils of another, and that the song was for communicating with spirits. The dancer stopped, picked up an open-topped box with a wooden handle and small objects inside, and extended it toward us, presumably offering us the drug. My guide waved him away and returned me to the river.

Tribal villages proliferated as we neared the mouth of the Brazo Casiquiare. On February 29 the latter joined the Rio Negro. Both were a half kilometer wide, of the same translucent black. We now had Colombia on the right bank again. On the left bank was San Carlos del Rio Negro, administrative center for this remote part of Venezuela.

San Carlos didn't have internet or a restaurant, but it did have yet another *Guardia Nacional* post and naval base. The naval *comandante,* a fastidious man with a golden retriever puppy, invited us into his office. He fondly reminisced about living in Alabama as a teenager while his father attended F-16 flight school. He showed us his cherished photos of Epcot Center and Disney World. He went on for hours in a curious balance between friendliness and tension. He seemed torn

Sugarloaf on the Rio Negro

UP THE ORINOCO,

between Chavez's xenophobic demagoguery and regret that Venezuela was becoming isolated. He evinced no ambivalence toward the Colombian navy, however. They had their own base just across the river. "They come over here and goose their engines as they go past, just to provoke us!" he scowled. "The scoundrels!"

A couple days later our GPS indicated that we had left Venezuela. Ginny high-fived me. "Adios assholes!" she bellowed, waving merrily at the final *Guardia Nacional* post. She had come to doubt if we would ever get out of there.

It was March 2, 2012, and we were in Brazil! It was forested, flat with isolated sugarloaf mountains. When not raining it was hot. The river was at mid-height and rising. The banks were often inundated forests. There were palms with upward-radiating fronds and hardwoods with buttress roots. Vines hung from the trees, their tips dragging in the river current. The people, mostly indigenous, drove dugout canoes powered by motors with long propeller shafts angling from the stern down into the water. The settlements had plank-built homes, stuccoed churches, and stands of banana trees.

One campsite description will suffice for many. Where the river squeezed through a rocky defile, behind a hemisphere of igneous rock covered with forest and fluffy duff, we found a small, semicircular cove. Its walls were of the same smooth rock. We tied to a root and pulled ourselves up to explore on foot. We had been seeing the same geology since the Orinoco River, but here the immense rainfall caused trees to root in the bedrock and a deep leaf litter to form, like a soft mattress. As we settled in for the night gentle eddies wafted *Thurston* left and right. A pink dolphin hunted nearby as the setting sun turned the clouds pink and blue.

We passed through an archipelago of forested islands interspersed with riffles where the river dropped over low ledges. We watched as the GPS's latitude readout slowly ran down to S 00 °00.000': the Equator!

On the left bank lay São Gabriel da Cachoeira (Saint Gabriel of the Waterfall). Above the fall wooden boats crowded the shoreline, many of them roofed and inhabited by large families. Boats loaded with fish and yucca were arriving while others loaded with cooking oil and bags of rice were heading upriver.

The equator, Rio Negro

We landed next to a barge serving cane liquor. Friendly drunks held out their hands to be shaken. It was like squeezing sponges: soft and wet! There were cars in the streets. At government offices we were politely escorted through the rigorous Brazilian entry procedures. Portuguese sounded totally different from Spanish: soft, lisping, nasal. We began a Portuguese language course on our laptop. The music was different too, more varied and interesting. We exchanged leftover Venezuelan *bolívares* and Colombian *pesos* for Brazilian *reais,* pronounced "hay-ice," accent on the ice.

We found an internet shop and started mapping the thousand river kilometers leading to Manaus. Though we represented shorelines with only about a click per kilometer, rapidly tracing our route via the satellite images, the task took twenty-five hours. Most of the way the river contained at least one long, sharp-ended island. In some regions vegetation and water intermingled in vast swamps, visually fascinating but hard to map. What proportion of green to blue should qualify as the boundary between land and river? In the river's undulating shapes could be discerned its slow writhing over time. In places parallel sloughs echoed the river's meanders. There were islands with lakes inside, channels that tapered to nothing as they stabbed into land masses, and dozens of converging tributaries, some with their own delta archipelagos congesting the main river.

In 1981 Don and Dana Starkell portaged their canoe around the São Gabriel *cachoeira* (see *Paddle to the Amazon*), but for us it was navigable, barely. We scouted it from shore. Just below our tie-up the river compressed from a mile in width to a mere quarter mile. At first there was whitewater along the bank and the middle was safe. Then the water by the bank became safe while the middle was occupied by the main *cachoeira,* a white mass where the river dropped eight feet. Ginny, though scared, chose to accompany me, "in case you need superhuman assistance," she said. Upon shoving off we angled upstream so as to maintain longitudinal station while crossing to the middle. It was black and boiling with upsurges and whirlpools! Then we angled back to the granite bank and sped down a swath of unbroken water. We got up to 23.6 kilometers per hour, then found ourselves swirling and bobbing in a quiet bay. But it wasn't over. For twenty kilometers the river flowed through rocky islands then compressed once more, mightily. Powering with our motor we bumped through a series of white corduroy waves, right down the middle! I loved it, Ginny hated it.

Thereafter the current was mild. The globular granite subsided until only flatland remained. The forest edge was a verdant wall. Branches covered with leafy vines extended well out over the river. There were vertical stalks with tiny white flowers in a "zipper" pattern and vines with leaves like elephant ears. The water was fresh and cool. Due to the tannic acid that darkened it there were no mosquitoes. In Panama and Colombia we'd hurried to avoid the December winds. In Venezuela we'd rushed to escape the clutches of the socialist Big Brother. For once we weren't in a hurry!

Our first indulgence was to ascend a randomly-selected tributary called the Rio Cauaburí. About the size of Washington State's Skagit River, its watershed is within the *Parque Nacional do Pico da Neblina,* named for Brazil's highest point, on the Venezuelan border. We motored as close to the bank as possible to minimize current, weaving in and out to avoid branches. We connected the steering lines, left the

Below the rapids at São Gabriel, Brazil

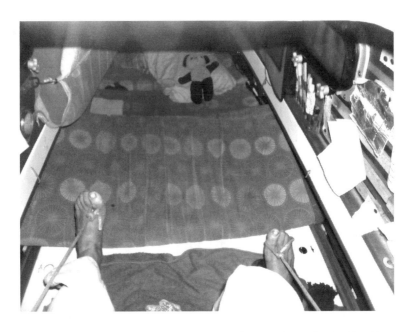

Steering with toes, lines running to fairleads on either side of tiller. I am seated in the companionway with a good view forward over the cabin top.

awning up to shelter us from the intermittent sun and rain, and had great fun conning our miniature ship while seated in the companionway.

After a couple hours we arrived at a cataract too fast to climb. Here a slough led into partly-inundated jungle. Lifting a few branches we squeezed inside. Now under the forest canopy, no wall of leaves separated us from the land. We explored, minding our track with a compass. There were small palm trees covered with long spines. Ants crawled up our legs and bit us if we lingered in the wrong place. The forest was walkable except where big trees had fallen, opening a hole to the sun and allowing dense shrubs to grow. Overhead a copper-colored monkey returned our stare. We found a cinnamon-colored tarantula on a rotten stump and a small mantis-like stick bug. Then a cloudburst hit, and the leafy forest floor soon puddled from the intensity of the rain. We stayed there two days and never got our clothes dried out! No people came by, but once a river otter examined us while chomping a fish, his big, round head protruding from the water. We felt isolated yet safe.

Hiking a forest trail, towing Thurston by hand, Rio Negro.

The remoteness overwhelmed us. Since Puerto Ayacucho the towns had been far apart with no connecting roads. There were native villages tucked away up various streams but most of Amazonia is simply uninhabited. The hummingbirds delighted us while our failure to see leopards frustrated us. In wilderness travel is there always some-place even more remote that you can't reach? With the right gear could one hike into a land where sloths can be cuddled, and spotted agoutis minutely observed? When if not now would we penetrate nature's innermost secret? We talked about leaving *Thurston's* sailing rig in Manaus and building a roomier canvas enclosure. We daydreamed of following the Rio Japurá into Colombia, or climbing the Madeira into Bolivia. We even fantasized about getting a bigger boat, having a kid, and becoming fluvial beekeepers. But what about our families, friends, professions, possessions? Would we lose our old senses of belonging? Would the wanderlust wane?

Resuming our descent of the Rio Negro we rowed and motored into mild headwinds. With the awning up clothing was optional. Some-times the river was so wide we couldn't see land on the other side. (We call these "sea horizons.") The flooding was everywhere. Often there was no land on which to walk, but rowing with a sliding seat exercises the whole body. The narrower channels abounded in lime-green parrots and macaws, both the scarlet and blue types. They flew in groups and were very vocal during the day. At night monkeys howled, cicadas whirred, frogs "croaked" in strange new ways, and varied bird calls reverberated through the forest.

The river was about twenty-five feet above its dry-season level. This allowed us to camp under heavy canopy in drowned forests. Fist-sized "acorns" often splashed down around us. Crimson bean pods adorned certain trees like Christmas ornaments. Some held Brazil nuts; they resemble cannon balls until their outer cases are broken apart, yielding nuts shaped like orange sections. Other times we anchored in the open among sparse trees. They must have been quite tall but we saw only their tops, so they looked small.

Sleeping tied to a tree precluded anchor problems, but exposed us to another hazard. One night *Thurston* accidentally floated into con-tact with a drowned tree. In the morning we found the boat crawling with desperate small ants! They had been "treed" as the river rose and would die off unless they found another home, such as *Thurston*. We spent two hours washing them off and smashing them. After that we tied bow and stern lines to opposing trees, tying off to underwater branches so insects couldn't enter via our mooring lines. At about 7:00 a.m. honey bees would swarm our masts and rigging, presumably to build a new nest, but they dissipated when we got underway, and never stung us. We tolerated spiders and crickets.

Rio Negro riverboat

Sometimes we passed a paddled dugout, a planked canoe with a "stick-out motor," a barge, or a wooden, triple-decker river boat. We saw fish traps along the bank looking rather like half-submerged outhouses made from slender poles lashed close together. Here and there trees had been cut, milled with chain saws, and the lumber removed. The wood was red and heavier than water. Every few days we passed towns where staples like rice and coffee could be bought: Santa Isabel, Barcelos, Moura, Novo Airão. In these locales we moored alongside families whose boats had thatched roofs, removable side tarps, wheel steering, and fantail sterns. They were poor but happy *mestizos* with naked kids and plenty of hammocks. Like them we washed our laundry in the river and festooned our boat with it to dry. The indigenous communities along this stretch had Entry Prohibited signs, so we didn't learn much about them.

Five days out of São Gabriel we entered the Anavilhanas, the world's biggest fluvial archipelago. They were a profusion of slender islands, as many as ten abreast, currently submerged except for the middle and upper reaches of their trees. They were up to fifty kilometers long. On satellite photos they look like emerald ribbons streaming in a current, but on a colossal scale. Many were bulbous with interior lakes. One evening we followed a channel leading inside an island. Here we found a lake. There was no current here but it was too large to anchor just anywhere, so we found a cove. We slept in a cove, in a lake, on an island, in a river!

When we exited these islands the river was four kilometers wide, fifty feet deep. Because the sky was usually overcast, the water's commonest mood was steel gray, oily smooth. Cutting the corner on a bend entailed a diagonal crossing that took two hours. In this interval a rainstorm packed with lightning and black clouds was likely to pass over, blinding us and kicking up waves.

Thirteen days out of São Gabriel we began a side trip up the Rio Branco, a major tributary coming in from the north. With no particular goal we explored it for three days, camping in side channels and hiking in the jungle. Our only human interaction was at a village of thirteen homes where a man had a canoe containing Brazil nuts. They were broken free of their outer husks and loaded in sacks. We still had an empty gasoline jug left over from our ascent of the Orinoco. I offered it to him with a reciprocating gesture toward his nuts, my Portuguese being insufficient to do more. Understanding immediately he took the jug and gave me a bag weighting about ten pounds. It took us weeks to eat them all!

Anchoring around forest I always worried that our Danforth might snag on a root or branch, and finally it did. One morning it didn't budge an inch; I would have to swim down to it. My lead line showed thirty-five feet of depth. I cleated the rode snug and descended head-first with the rope in my hand. From three feet on down it was pitch black, hence the name Negro. I wore my mask out of habit, but I might as well have just kept my eyes closed. The depth was at the limit of my breath-holding ability. It took several attempts to reach the anchor and free it.

On April 6 we began passing red river banks, then tall buildings and mega-yachts under huge boathouses. The river corridor had remained relatively untouched until just before its merger with the Amazon. Here, on the north bank, sat Manaus, a city of two million people. In Novo Airão we had met British Peter and South African Louise, who had come up the Amazon in their famous motor-sailer, the *Passagemaker*. They were the first sailboat we had seen coming down the river and we were the first they'd seen coming up. "When you get to Manaus, tie up with us at Erin Shipyard," Peter had said.

We found Erin Shipyard on a tract of sloping red clay just before a long, tall bridge. Petroleum barges were being built under big sheds. Ferry boats in red primer lay on ways. Welding torches sparked here and there. On all sides workers in bright orange coveralls clanged and clambered over vessels. Equipment and timbers lay everywhere. Floating dry docks lay moored alongshore. A crane held the stern of a tugboat aloft while men worked on its propellers. We moored where a floating workshop had left a strip of sheltered water between itself and the shore.

Peter and Louise of the *Passagemaker* had left, but Francisco, the manager, welcomed us. We became fast friends with him and his wife, Berlane. He had worked in the marine industry around São Paulo. Berlane's father owned the shipyard. When they married Francisco became the manager. They lived in a tall condominium a kilometer or two away. Francisco drove us on important errands, such as to facilitate customs for a shipment we had coming. The office was in the ultramodern industrial district, which houses hundreds of assembly plants, including the world's largest motorcycle factory! Even the bureaucrats were helpful. At one point Francisco got out and talked with a man sweeping the sidewalk. The subject seemed to be changes occurring in that neighborhood.

"How did you happen to know him?" asked Ginny when Francisco got back behind the wheel.

"Oh, I don't know him. In Brazil we are all friends. We can always talk to each other." Indeed! We would ultimately spend eighteen months in Brazil, and we always sensed that fraternity, that harmony.

Mostly we got around on foot. We would first hike up the long, steep driveway from the shipyard to the plateau, then catch a bus to the Centro Antigo (Old Center). There the buildings largely dated from the late 1800s when Manaus was rich from the rubber boom. The facades were molded in a heavy, neoclassical style. On the waterfront was a sprawling public market. One shed the size of an auditorium contained nothing but green plantains! The produce was hand-trucked there from rough-hewn cargo boats along the grimy quay. Up and down the waterfront tour-boat operators hawked rides. High-speed ferries streaked across the river. Floating gas stations lay offshore. A passenger terminal accommodated a cruise ship and a score of big river boats. The eating establishments offered a wealth of unfamiliar dishes and juices.

Manaus

When we returned to the shipyard it was often very hot, but the floating workshop sheltered us from the afternoon sun, and served as an excellent diving platform. The current was mild, the water clean and fresh. Living in the shipyard seemed too good to be true! Surely, we thought, someone would worry about security or safety, yet these subjects never came up. We were totally free, totally un-hassled.

Diving off the barge we moored to in Manaus

We stayed ten weeks, conducting repairs, waiting for our package, and seeking hard-to-find items. Our affairs often took us through slums with narrow, winding streets. Through each ravine ran an open sewer. The two-story shacks pressed in close, on stilts if necessary to avoid flooding. There were no Yellow Pages, no bus schedules, no street name signs or address numbers. Businesses didn't post their hours. Restaurants had no menus. Vendors didn't bother with price labels. Nor were our English or Spanish of much use. The lack of written information forced us to converse. We accelerated our Rosetta Stone lessons. We immersed ourselves in the culture, so our progress was rapid. And the Brazilians made our apprenticeship a pleasure by being warm and friendly.

One day, while walking through a neighborhood called Lirio do Vale (Lily of the Valley), we passed along a walled garden. Over an elaborate gate were the words União do Vegetal (Union of the Vegetable). "What the heck?" I wondered out loud. The gate being ajar, we peeked in. A handsome young man just inside noticed us. He beckoned us in. "We are a Christian group," he explained. "In our sessions we take a special tea made of Amazonian plants. If you would like to try it you'd be most welcome. Just come back Tuesday night at eight o'clock."

On the appointed evening Ginny was tired so I walked the three kilometers alone. The grounds were now inhabited by about forty men wearing green smocks and white trousers, and a smaller number of women. They were gathered on a covered patio around a table on which stood a white ceramic urn. Five leaders sat to one side of the table. Everyone else sat opposite except that I and three other newcomers were placed to the right of the leaders. The chairs were comfortable. One by one we were served a glass of tea called ayahuasca. It was extracted from the leaves of a tree and the sap from a vine, both of which grew on the grounds. It was bitter and pungent. A chairman opened the service. He and others gave short talks. Members stood, were recognized, and asked questions. Brief answers were given. Sometimes someone would chant. There were long periods of meditation during which soothing music was played from a CD.

At nine o'clock we were offered a second cup. Having felt no effect I accepted. Soon my body felt wiry. Closing my eyes I saw colorful, evolving patterns suggestive of plant growth, or zeppelins, or skyscrapers. The images were pixilated like a TV screen. I noticed certain words being repeated: *espiritu, vegetal,* Gabriel, Soloman. I fell into a dream but could wake up at any time by opening my eyes.

At eleven-thirty the ceremony ended. People lingered, chatting in good humor. Some ate. My intoxication lasted until a man sitting beside me emitted a sharp odor. Suddenly I had to vomit. Fortunately a restroom was nearby. I was instantly sober! "It's normal," someone said. I was given a ride back to the shipyard. I woke the next day feeling refreshed. They invited me back, but my curiosity was satisfied.

Manaus is a rich civilization, yet it is an island in a sea of rivers. The Amazon isn't just the biggest river in the world. Rather, it's altogether unique. It's bigger than the world's second, third, fourth, fifth, sixth, seventh, and eighth largest rivers combined! The Mississippi is smaller than the Negro and has less than one twelfth the flow of the combined Amazon. Due to water obstacles no roads connect Manaus with Brazil's main population belt, which begins a thousand miles to the southeast. That isolation is heightened during the high water, which in turn is a function of the seasons. From Mexico through Venezuela the rainy season is from June to November. In the southern hemisphere it is from November to June. It was now June. We had passed through the Llanos during their dry season and had arrived in the Amazon as its rains were tapering off. But the runoff accumulates faster than it can discharge, so the highest floods come while the precipitation is tapering off. And this year the floods reached an all-time high. In the Centro Antigo businesses stacked sandbags around their entrances. Cars couldn't drive there but elevated walkways were erected along the streets so people could still get around.

It was during this time of flooding that we discovered one urban gem. We offer it as a sample. One day we were shopping for materials for a new awning in an inner-city neighborhood called Educandos. From there one crosses over a tall bridge to return to the Centro Antigo. In doing so we noticed that the shacks, docks, and floating businesses that blanket the riverfront continued under the bridge itself. Descending to river level we saw that informal structures had been built around the massive abutments. The bridge overhead protected them from rain and sun. Crude plank walkways snaked from shack to shack. Some habitations had a foot of water inside yet they remained occupied. In some buildings the downstairs was a combination bar/restaurant/store. Typically these had seating for two or three customers and shelves offering cooking oil, candles, and similar wares. Laundry lines ran from upstairs windows to convenient attachment points. We sat at one of the "bars" and split a tall bottle of cold Brahma beer. Men drank quietly. Women cooked. Children darted in and out. Dogs, cats, chickens, and ducks inhabited whatever ledges they could find. The planks were wide enough for one person or animal at a time. People had top priority, followed by dogs, then cats, ducks, and chickens. As we returned to shore (a relative term) a dog accidentally nudged a fighting cock into the water. A passerby casually reached down, grabbed it by the shoulders of its wings, set it back on the plank, and continued on his way.

By June 14 thousands of homes were flooded, but floods don't bother sailors. Our chores were done. It was time for another decision. Should we sail down the Amazon and return home via the Atlantic? Or prolong the trip yet again by borrowing the idea of Virgilio, our travel-guide friend in Puerto Ayacucho? He had said it is possible to ascend the Madeira, which comes into the Amazon from the south, and portage from its headwaters to the Paraguay, which flows into the Paraná, which flows into the Atlantic at Buenos Aires. We mapped a route that looked feasible. From Buenos Aires we could either follow the Atlantic coast north or ascend and descend a different set of rivers, reaching the mouth of the Amazon by a different route. We chose to adopt Virgilio's idea and decide the return route later. With this intention we motored from the shipyard to the confluence of the Negro and Amazon rivers, only a few kilometers distant, and continued down the main stem of the Amazon. At the mouth of the Madeira, two hundred kilometers further, we would turn right.

Route

Portage

Chapter 6

UP THE MADEIRA, DOWN THE PARAGUAY

The black waters of the Rio Negro and tan of the Amazon mixed but slowly. On the banks were half-immersed houses, the Amazon being in flood. At dusk we motored into a forest and tied to a tree within view of ocean-going freighters on their way to Manaus. A current streamed us away from the tree.

When Ginny slid open a floorboard to get dinner ingredients she started. The normally dry bilge contained three inches of water, just an inch shy of flooding our bins! After bailing we found a pinprick hole through the hull just below the waterline on the starboard quarter. Before leaving Manaus we had tied up at the downtown seawall to get produce at the market. The boat had bumped against a sharp projection. I had neglected to check for damage. We kept ahead of it by bailing. The next morning we found a solid bank to work on. Positioning *Thurston* under a tree we ran a line from the affected area to an overhead branch. Hoisting upward we raised the hole above the water line. I patched the outside with epoxy and fiberglass. Ginny squirmed into an impossibly tight space and patched it from the inside.

This stretch of the Amazon was at least twice as voluminous as the Negro, yet it didn't seem so. Perhaps at this scale relative size is hard to distinguish. On the third day we turned right at the Rio Madeira. We hoped to ascend it to Bolivia. We would then take its tributary, the Guaporé, along the Brazil/Bolivia border to its head of navigation at Vila Bela. From there we would transport to the Paraguay/Paraná river system, which we would descend to Argentina.

Filling our one-liter fuel bottles in a town on the Rio Madeira.
The Honda motor only holds a liter, so we refilled with these.

We had only eighty days left on our Brazilian visas, so we motored from sunrise to sunset every day. At first the Madeira was so big we had sea horizons. Further upstream it narrowed. Perhaps the flooding was a phenomenon of the Amazon and Negro rivers which merely backed up into the Madeira, because the flooding decreased as we went up. Eventually only muddy banks were exposed. The trees become shorter, indicating less rainfall. Each homestead was a gap in the forest with a planked house on stilts, a few banana trees, farm animals, dogs, kids, and a canoe out front. We passed river boats and tugs pushing tows of up to six barges. The upper Madeira also had hundreds of *garimpeiro* barges: wooden flatboats that anchored in the river and sucked up bottom sediment with a thick hose to extract gold dust. They often tied up side-by-side while they worked.

We minimized contrary current by hugging the shore, swerving to avoid snags. Leaves and twigs littered our decks whenever we brushed against vegetation. Lilies often crowded out from shore, requiring detours. The person not steering would make sandwiches, sew, etc. Every few days we passed a town. They had paved streets but no roads connecting them to other towns. The heart of each was the municipal floating dock where passengers waited for boats and goods were hurried to their destinations. Stevedores carried refrigerators and bicycles ashore via wobbly gangplanks while plantains moved in the opposite direction.

We always wondered how long the Honda two-horsepower motor could be ran at three-quarter throttle. On June 24 we found out. It had started using oil, which is bad in an engine whose oil capacity is only a quarter of a liter. We topped it up frequently but not frequently enough. It made a bad sound and stopped. No compression. Whatever was broken we weren't going to find the parts within a thousand miles.

We decided to buy another motor and continue upstream, so we rowed back down to a line of *garimpeiro* barges we had passed. Twelve of them lay at anchor in the full stream of the river, secured side-by-side to each other. Each had two horizontal wooden capstans. With one the operator jigged the suction head up and down, working it deeper into the bottom. The effluent gushed out of a large hose onto a carpeted ramp. The carpet caught the flecks of gold. Every half hour or so, when the hole became too deep, somebody would blow a whistle and they would all crank the second capstan, which pulled them closer to their anchors. They would then re-lower the suction heads and start new holes. Each morning they turned off their engines long enough to remove the carpet and agitate it in a tank of water and mercury. They then collected the gold dust at the bottom of the tank. The *garimpeiros* worked in two-man teams, twenty-four hours a day on six-hour shifts. The off-duty man slept in a bunk in a thatched attic. The diesel engines powering the suction heads rumbled constantly.

In the Amazon small boats don't use outboards. Instead they mount a *rabeta* on their transom. This means "little tail," but "long-tail" would be more descriptive. A little-tail is a 5.5 horsepower gas motor with a long propeller shaft bolted to its crankshaft. The entirety angles down and aft to immerse the propellor. It sits on a universal pivot and is steered via a tiller. One of the *garimpeiros* offered to sell us his but it failed the test drive, conking out repeatedly.

Garimpeiros (gold dredgers), Rio Madeira, Brazil

After two days a *garimpeiro* took me in his skiff to speak with a boat passing upriver. They were Catholic missionaries who provided scheduled services in tiny communities along the river. The leader was a jeans-clad nun in her thirties. "We will gladly tow you to Humaitá," she said. "That is where our diocese is. But it will take us four days to get there." We accepted, bade good-bye to our *garimpeiro* friends, and connected the boats with our good tow line. She was the *Edigio Vigano*, a stately one-story river boat. To protect *Thurston's* bow I sawed off a four-foot length of a common local "tree" resembling a ten-inch-diameter green onion. This I lashed to *Thurston's* bow to serve as a fender. It cushioned blows whenever the *Edigio Vigano* abruptly cut its engines.

The nun was from Santa Catarina state in southern Brazil, where the people are of European descent. The priest was a tall, jovial African immigrant. A competent skipper and cook completed the team. Below deck a low-ceilinged engine compartment ran the length of the vessel. On deck she had a salon, three small cabins, pantry, galley, and head. Once we were sure *Thurston* was being safely towed we came aboard the *Edigio Vigano* and shared meals with them. The boat was clean and orderly.

Catholic missionary boat that towed us to Humaitá, Brazil

In the following days we stopped at nine communities, each consisting of five to ten wooden houses. The staple food was manioc, the crumbly kernels of which they roasted in a five-foot-diameter pan over a fire, stirring with long paddles. The churches were small, doorless structures. The attendees, mostly mothers and children, were largely Amerindian. The friendly priest would don his vestments and talk about the changes occurring in the world. "Some of these changes are good," he said. "For example, America has a black president now. Did you know that? But other changes are bad. Beware! Rely upon the guidance of the Church!" He advised them *not* to use condoms. They apparently didn't, because most families had eight or nine children.

To get from their boat to the village in the background the missionaries relied on canoe rides across this cut-off channel of the Madeira River.

The *Edigio Vigano's* plastic nesting chairs were all broken, so when we got to Humaitá we bought them six new ones as our thank-you. Then the skipper showed us to a shop where for $775 we bought a little-tail and had a mount fabricated. It attached where the rudder normally went. We stowed the broken Honda and the rudder on *Thurston's* narrow side decks, where we had stowed our auxiliary fuel tanks on the upper Orinoco.

Three days later, on July 3, 2012, we arrived in Porto Velho, a city of 400,000. Huge barges were moored along the bank. One was being loaded with soy beans via a chute that emitted a plume of chaff. At the small-boat waterfront laborers were paving a new plaza. Brazil's highway network extends to Porto Velho, so finally we were connected to the rest of the country. We started looking for transportation around the dams and rapids that block navigation between Porto Velho and Guajará-Mirim. The manager of a boating store connected us with the owner of a pickup truck and trailer. We agreed to pay him about $475 for the move.

We hauled out at a boat ramp. The road was about four hundred kilometers long and badly pot-holed. Tall termite mounds studded the surrounding plains. The land became noticably drier as we proceeded. Guajará-Mirim was dusty and spread-out. The driver unloaded us next to a ramp. We kept *Thurston* on land another day in order to install a skeg. We needed it because without the rudder *Thurston* wanted to swerve left and right under little-tail power. I just carved a slab of wood and epoxied it on. Then we launched *Thurston* in the Rio Guaporé, a tributary of the Madeira.

Adding a skeg to Thurston in Guajará-Mirim, Brazil

We were still in Brazil but we now had Bolivia on the opposite bank. Brazil has high import duties, Bolivia doesn't, so we loaded up on cheap fuel smuggled from across the river. That night, as we slept at the landing, blacked-out boats kept sneaking in, unloading merchandise, then quickly departing. I peeked occasionally. One load consisted of nothing but wooden tables and chairs.

On July 9 we began the second half of our grueling upstream leg. On the Madeira we had travelled southwest 1,056 river kilometers. Now we would ascend the Guaporé 1,462 kilometers southeast to the head of navigation at Vila Bela. The boats above the rapids were flat-bottomed, diesel-powered barges made from heavy timbers. Some were open, others had boxy houses of one or two stories.

The little-tail took getting used to. It was loud, and it vibrated so violently the bolts holding the tiller in place kept breaking. The long appendage was awkward in tight spaces. It was also very sensitive to weight distribution, wanting to turn in the direction of the lighter side of the boat. One day, as we rounded a sharp turn with the throttle wide-open, the whole motor jumped up out of its swivel and landed in the cockpit beside me! We kept it tied down after that.

After a week we reached the town of Costa Marques. We refueled there and again at Porto Rolim. The towns kept getting smaller, the river traffic lighter. The Guaporé meandered deeply, often doubling the straight-line distance. Muddy banks gave way to sand. When sandbars became a problem we probed for depth with our boat-hook. Our GPS map told us which way to go at forks. Its speed readout helped us estimate current, useful for deciding how to position ourselves laterally in the river. We averaged four knots made good.

A cold front hit! We were only twelve degrees south of the equator and 550 feet above sea level, yet a frigid wind blew off the Andes, two hundred miles away to the southwest. We wore all our clothes and slept with the cabin hatch closed. The air smelled like autumn.

One morning the little-tail motor had gas and spark but still wouldn't fire. That stumped me. Fortunately we were near a low-tech Bolivian naval base, so we rowed there. It consisted of the usual dirt boat landing and some barracks. The *comandante* assigned a cheerful young mechanic to us. This fellow tinkered with me all day, breaking for breakfast and lunch. When the sun got hot we worked on an upside-down boat under a shade tree. He never despaired of finding the problem. Finally he found a sticky intake valve. "But I don't have any emery cloth," he lamented.

"I've got some!" I said triumphantly, and fetched a piece.

"The American has everything!" he laughed. He soon had the motor running. I thanked the sailors by giving them rides.

*Little-tail motor in action, giving rides to sailors at
a Bolivian naval base on the Rio Guaporé*

Later the propeller-shaft housing gave trouble. It consisted of a six-foot-long steel tube with four evenly-spaced wooden bushings holding the shaft in alignment. By July 21 the bushings had become worn, so in the town of Pimenteiros d'Oeste we had a woodworker replace them.

A black fly with clear wing-tips began biting our feet in the day. When darkness fell the mosquitoes came out, so we hurriedly snapped a mosquito net around on the cabin hatch and hung another over the cockpit so I could sit there while Ginny cooked. Moths lived in our noodles and weevils had to be sifted from our flour. We welcomed certain visitors, however. New species of butterflies and dragonflies kept touching down. In the evening "mole crickets" were attracted to our headlamps. Two inches long, they wriggled and scurried incessantly, every now and then executing a high back flip. On one such flip Ginny swears she saw him catch a mosquito in mid-air! His aft half is similar to that of a cricket but he has mole-like "forearms," presumably either for burrowing or for catching mosquitoes.

The further we got upriver the more wildlife we saw: turtles, alligators, monkeys, river otters, dolphins, and capybaras by the dozen! The latter is a 150-pound rodent with a body like a hog, a square head, and rich brown fur. They sat on the low marshy banks munching vegetation. We now saw green kingfishers in addition to the red-bellied ones. Storks, bitterns, cormorants, roseate spoonbills! New species of hawk and owl! We wished we had a bird book and fully functional camera; only the upper right-hand corner of our camera's screen worked now, so we had little to go on for framing our shots. We slept in marshy bays, where all night we heard splashes, sighs, chortles, chirps, peeps, and grunts. We also needed a device to identify animals by their sounds!

Bedrock occasionally appeared through the green mantle. We skirted to the north of a Bolivian mountain range. Masses of filamentous vine cocooned tall bushes among the swamp grass. The vines sometimes died, leaving what looked like haystacks. The river shrank to as narrow as fifty yards, then twenty yards. The scenery changed more rapidly. We no longer saw native dwellings. For a while sport fishermen in small aluminum boats were common, then nothing.

By July 25 the Guaporé was a minor stream gushing through forest, swamp, and cattle range. The bends were so sharp we had to muscle the little-tail hard over. Sometimes we miscalculated and crashed into the bank. Rounding a final island we saw buildings: Vila Bela da Santissima Trinidade (Beautiful Village of the Most Sacred Trinity)! Here the stream issued from the Mato Grosso *Pantanal,* the world's biggest swamp. We had completed our ascent! Just as the Brazo Casiquiare marked the end of our time on the Orinoco, we were now at the southern rim of the Amazon basin, the world's largest. We had transited Amazonia from north to south. Now we arranged transport to the world's second largest basin in terms of land area, that of the Paraná/Paraguay. The two basins adjoin at the world's largest swamp, the Mato Grosso *Pantanal.*

"Let's only go to the world's largest things from now on," I suggested.

"As long as they're right next to each other, why not," Ginny agreed. "And by the way, I've been getting morning sickness." (More on that later.)

Within two days we had arranged for transportation to the Rio Paraguay. We unloaded *Thurston* to lighten her. This time we had no trailer, just a heavy-duty pickup truck upon which the owner installed a bit of wooden cradling. Seven men slid the bow up over the cab, the stern angling down behind. For $370 the driver took us three hundred kilometers to the city of Cáceres.

Haul-out at Vila Bela da Santissima Trinidade

It took four hours to get to Cáceres, a small Brazilian city on the Rio Paraguay, a major tributary of the Paraná. After unloading we walked for half a day in search of food that appealed to Ginny's heightened sense of smell, to no avail. She was sick but ambulatory! Cáceres being the gateway to the *Pantanal,* the waterfront was lined with aluminum skiffs and three-story "hotel-boats" offering sport-fishing excursions. We planned to ride the Paraguay south through the *Pantanal,* transiting the Brazilian states of Mato Grosso ("Big Bush") and Mato Grosso do Sul ("Big Bush of the South"). Our next town would be Corumbá, 850 river kilometers downstream.

We left Cáceres on July 29, 2012. What a relief to be travelling downstream again! Swamp soon swallowed us. The river meandered deeply, sometimes nearly reattaching to itself. We saw no soil, just water, plants, and wildlife, especially otters, capybaras, and monkeys. Now and then something bellowed in the adjoining lakes and marshes. Alligators? Bullfrogs? We saw new species of birds, including a busy fellow with a body the size of a golf ball and a bright red head who often rode the drifting hyacinths (free-floating lilies) catching insects.

Another cold front hit. This was beginning to make sense because we had by now distanced ourselves a good deal from the equator and this was the South American winter. Ginny had another theory. "It's those penguins down in Antarctica flapping their flippers, blowing that cold wind up here," she averred. At least the cold ameliorated the evening and morning mosquito problem.

Clumps of water hyacinth constricted the channel by sticking to tree snags and adhering to the adjoining plant communities, where grasses and leafed succulents stood chest-high above river-level. Short trees grew in patches. Birds flew abundantly. The only people we saw were those inhabiting the hotel-boats. They would anchor at some secluded spot, like small cruise ships lurking in the swamp. Each morning the guests would disperse, three or four to an aluminum skiff, with a guide driving. All day they would fish. In the evenings they reconvened in the air-conditioned comfort of the mother ship.

The Mato Grosso Pantanal, world's largest swamp

Our regimen was less luxurious but pleasant nonetheless. Upon loosing ourselves from whatever branch we had tied to for the night we rowed a couple hours for exercise. Given the lack of land we especially relished the pushing action of our legs in the sliding seat. We would then motor the rest of the day. This too was peaceful because we did so at low throttle, burning only one pint of fuel per hour. If it was hot we put up the awning. While one of us steered the other might bathe on the foredeck in the afternoon sun, dipping the bailer into the river and dumping the contents over our bodies. The boat's motion induced a breeze, which evaporated the water, chilling us delightfully.

On our third day in the *Pantanal* we touched onto its western edge: a range of sharp, low mountains running north and south along the Bolivian border. Parking *Thurston* in a cut-off slough we climbed 1500 vertical feet through thorny scrub and sharp boulders to a vantage point. It being the dry season the hills were a dusty brown in contrast to the blues and greens of the *Pantanal,* which stretched two hundred miles eastward. The swamp, being more water than land, conformed perfectly to the curvature of the earth.

Our hike was for reconnaissance as well as leg-stretching. Mapping the *Pantanal* had involved much guesswork. The satellite imagery showed a maze of filamentous sloughs. Sometimes the correct channel could be inferred, sometimes not. We had mapped all the serious contenders and hoped that the true river would reveal itself by its current. So far that had proved to be the case. But at the foot of the mountain range on which we stood lay another test: a chain of large lakes. Somehow the river coursed around or through them.

Again, current guided our path except in the lakes themselves. Here we motored through still water. We dropped the lead line a few times in search of channel depth but, in the event, the proper outlet was never hard to find. In a spot where the right-hand lakeshore was a rock wall we happened upon another reward as well: a set of ancient petroglyphs consisting of curved lines, concentrically nestled, with a dot at either end of each line. They had been carved by someone in a boat.

Hieroglyphics in the Pantanal

On our sixth day out of Cáceres the river entered a dry plain brightened with the pink blossoms of a large tree. Native dwellings appeared. Ginny, as always, became depressed that a wilderness sojourn was drawing to a close. Corumbá, southern gateway to the *Pantanal,* stood on a high plateau. At the seawall we moored among the work boats common to this stretch of the Paraguay: about thirty feet long, wooden, with a sharp bow and a boxy stern cabin. In the evenings teenagers thronged a beautiful plaza adjoining the waterfront. A sound system broadcast a medley of hits among which "I'm Sexy and I Know It" was unfortunately prominent. Vast fields across the river were being burnt causing ashes to sprinkle us like black snowflakes.

In this city of 110,000 inhabitants we found such necessities as a new fly-swatter (we had worn out our old one), earplugs, and Vaseline to lubricate the oarlocks. Across the border in Puerto Suarez, Bolivia, we bought a new Nikon digital with eighteen-power zoom! Our wildlife shots got better after that.

We now faced a bureaucratic dilemma. Our next country would be Paraguay which, like Brazil, requires that Americans get visas beforehand. In their website Paraguay claimed to have a consulate in Corumbá. This proved untrue. A lady at a tourism office made some calls for us. She found that the nearest place we could get visas would be in São Paulo, a thousand miles away, but that officials at the border *might* issue us a transit pass, meaning we wouldn't officially enter and couldn't legally go ashore. We decided to proceed on that basis. Since Corumbá was the last Brazilian city on our route we checked out of the country and got a naval clearance for Argentina, the country after Paraguay.

On August 12 we continued through a plain studded with chit palms. The tall *tuiuiu* stork with a black head and scarlet band around his neck stood passively on the bank like a wooden Indian. Barge tows up to four wide and five long now carried iron ore to smelters downriver. On the second day the west bank became Paraguayan soil. The first Paraguayan naval post had no boat, only a building with a guard out front. I approached him nervously. "Pardon me, but I am stopping to notify you that we are passing through your country. Are there any regulations we should be aware of?" I got this out haltingly in Spanish, which I hadn't spoken for six months.

"Welcome señor! No, here everyone crosses the river freely, and there are no navigation rules beyond the ordinary." At a subsequent post the *comandante* typed out a naval pass for us. That was the sum of our paperwork in Paraguay, where our passports were never stamped and no official ever approached us, but all responded courteously to our approach. What a pleasant surprise!

After five days with Brazil to left and Paraguay to right we entered Paraguay entirely. We averaged a hundred river kilometers a day. A pointy hill would pop up in the morning and by night we would be past it. In one stretch a dusty white mineral, perhaps limestone, was being mined from the tall riverbank, packed into sacks, and stowed into rusty boats. The Paraguayans lived in rough-hewn plank homes and *rowed* their planked dories, a means of propulsion strangely absent elsewhere in Latin America. Though most of the people were *mestizos*, they spoke among themselves an Indian language called Guarani, switching to Spanish for our benefit. They are the only country to have retained a Native American tongue as their official language.

With a friendly dog on a remote stretch of the hyancinth-choked Rio Paraguay. (Oddly, that hill in the background is an island, the river dividing around it. We had taken the right-hand channel.)

We were now far enough south of the equator that sail-able winds were frequent. Our transom hardware accepted either our Brazilian little-tail motor or our rudder. To switch from motoring to sailing took fifteen minutes. The trees tended to block the wind and the river bends necessitated constant sheet adjustments, but the favorable current eased any frustration.

In the small city of Concepción everyone enthusiastically drank *yerba mate*, an herbal tea, from a special leather-armored mug using an engraved silver straw incorporating a filter at its lower end. Ginny, unwilling to depart from her own morning ritual, scoured the market to find anyone able to prepare instant coffee. The vehicles were mostly horse-drawn carts and small motorcycles. The principle buildings were monumental antiques in a heavy Spanish style, with ridiculously tall doors and ceilings. The 10,000 Guarani note was worth only $2.30 U.S.; they had suffered crazy inflation at some point and never saw fit to remove the zeros by issuing a new currency, as most Latin American countries have done.

Asunción, Paraguay's capital and only large city, lay on high land on the left bank. The river traffic intensified, mostly rusty freighters. Tilting hulks lay abandoned along the bank. Rowing men retrieved fishing lines they had set the night before, each secured by a rock on the bottom and a plastic bottle on top. We passed a belt of shanties and tarp shelters, the refuse from which was dumped over the bank. Behind these rose skyscrapers. Turning left into a bay we found ourselves in the heart of the city. We moored under a busy passenger pier, tying off to pilings. Ginny stayed with the boat while I climbed up onto the pier and ventured through the thronged terminal and out into the street. No one questioned me.

I had only one mission: to gather cash for use in Argentina, which we would soon enter. Like Venezuela, Argentina maintained an artificial exchange rate vis-à-vis the dollar. We had deduced from internet research that we could stretch our funds by buying Argentine pesos in Paraguay, where the free market prevails. So at a cash machine I withdrew funds in the form of guaranis (their money is named after their language), then exchanged these for pesos. The net result was 6.1 pesos to the dollar. This would compare to 4.5 if we got pesos from a cash machine in Argentina. We also withdrew dollars for use in the

Argentine black market. That day and the next I withdrew to the daily limit allowed by our bank, hoping that would get us to Buenos Aires.

Before leaving Paraguay I couldn't resist investigating something we had noticed on Google Earth. On the right bank Paraguay meets Argentina along a clogged slough called the Pilcomayo River, a tributary of the Paraguay. On the Argentine side is the city of Clorinda. The Paraguayan side is rural except where a footbridge crossed over the Pilcomayo. Zooming way in we saw that the Paraguayan side of the footbridge was densely jammed with small buildings. What was going on there?

To find out we crossed the Paraguay and ascended the Pilcomayo, which was merely a swampy channel, to a low-density slum. Ginny stayed with the boat while I walked a kilometer along a street paved with broken rocks. Suddenly tarp-roofed stalls encroached upon the roadway. Inside the constriction was a chaotic gallery of shops. Men bent under the weight of huge bundles started passing me. Some carried impossibly tall stacks of eggs, the tiers separated by sheets of molded cardboard. Others carried bottled beer, as much as twenty cases each! Their bundles were expertly tied; these people did this for a living. Some carried their loads to a crowded bus stop, others into dark doorways. Obviously these were Argentine goods arriving in Paraguay, but I still hadn't found the footbridge.

Retracing my steps I found an entryway that was inconspicuous except for a high volume of people walking in and out. Inside were tiny shops hustling watches, cell phones, underwear, etc. The walls were splotched, the ceiling low. At the end of a long corridor I found myself on the footbridge. It was a hundred yards long. On the other side Clorinda was relatively affluent, with normal streets and building spacing. An Argentine official stood at his end of the footbridge. He wasn't demanding documents, so I walked into a new country unchecked! There was a regular highway border crossing only a couple miles away, so why did they haul all that stuff in by hand? Evidently only via the footbridge, in quantities small enough to manhandle, did the respective countries allow duty-free importation. Curiosity satisfied, and paranoid about being caught illegally in Argentina, I hustled back to Paraguay and to my patient wife.

The next day we descended the Paraguay to a ferry landing on the Argentine side. Here we found an office building full of armed men in neat tan uniforms with black ties. They pertained to a riverine unit of the *Prefectura Naval,* the Argentine coast guard. It being Saturday afternoon, the immigration and customs officials were gone for the weekend. We didn't mind waiting because it was too cold to travel. Grey clouds streaked across the sky. Those penguins were flapping their wings again! We shut ourselves up in the cabin and warmed it up with our body heat. Ease of heating is yet another advantage of small boats!

When Monday arrived the officials launched into our paperwork. They were friendly but obsessed with obtuse legalities. They made us sign a document promising, among other things, to sleep only in settled ports and present ourselves at all *Prefectura* stations along the way. That this would be highly inconvenient didn't concern them.

Warm weather returned. With Paraguay now on the left bank and Argentina on the right we entered a land still flat but green with early spring. On the banks were huge silos and conveyors for loading soybeans onto barges. We promptly violated the terms of our pass by sleeping in a marsh and ignoring *Prefectura* posts when no one was looking, with no ill result. It felt wrong to break a promise, but even they weren't very serious about it. They wanted to control us yet seemed disinclined to punish us for our violations, like they weren't on firm ground.

On our last night on the Paraguay River we stayed at a place called Puerto Bermejo. The "port" consisted of a gushing creek mouth ten feet wide. We poled ourselves fifty yards upstream then tied to a stake among some rowboats. The bank was steep. Above, a chubby *Prefectura Naval* guard sat on a chair beside a dirt road. He quickly rose to greet us. Behind him was a series of row-houses, half of which were in ruins.

"What happened to this town?" I asked.

"Bermejo is very old. It is declining now," he said. "The 1983 flood destroyed many of the houses."

A boy on horseback picked up a parcel from the store, a tall brick structure with no sign. A drunk got Ginny to take his picture with me. In the middle of town were low spots from which came little calls of descending pitch, like babies crying. "Frogs," said the drunk. The cemetery was calving off into the river. At the foot of a tall vertical bank broken vaults and headstones lay half-immersed in the brown current. Bones showed through torn metal caskets.

The next day, September 2, 2012, the Paraguay emptied into the much-larger Rio Paraná. Both sides of the river were in Argentina now. Twenty kilometers downstream of the confluence we stopped at Corrientes, a city of 250,000 on the left (east) bank. An ocean-going ship was being unloaded at a tall wharf. From the downstream end of the wharf streamed a line of two-story floating buildings. These served as breakwater for the local yacht club, whose docks were squeezed between them and the tall bank, like a canyon parallel to the shore. There were about fifty sail- and power-boats. The management introduced us to a fine Argentine tradition: the courtesy mooring! In the coming months we never lacked for nautical hospitality.

Our first errand was to find a clinic because Ginny was three months pregnant! We had decided that river life was so easy we could reproduce without undue disruption. Perhaps fighting the dark, swirling currents of the Rio Madeira had triggered a salmonid instinct, because that's where we conceived the blip that would become George. The ultrasound revealed something the size of a salamander dancing inside Ginny's womb. Given the country we were in, perhaps it was the tango. Depending on where we were at time of birth, our blip would be born either Argentine, Uruguayan, Paraguayan, or Brazilian.

The next task was to revive our two-horse outboard motor, broken down since the Rio Madeira. A mechanic took it apart. "These rings are cooked like spaghetti!" he said. "And the rod is broken from being fused onto the crankshaft. I can't get the parts from Honda because *la Presidenta* won't let us have dollars." He grimaced referring to then-President Christina Kirchner, who tried to prop up the peso by not allowing access to dollars. "But our aftermarket industry can make most things." He sent the crankshaft away for rehabilitation.

It took days to figure out how to adapt our cell phone and computer modem for use in Argentina, the technology and plans being very different. The buses only accepted coins which were acutely scarce. We used the pesos I had obtained in Asunción, and began supplementing them by selling our cash dollars to a shopkeeper who dabbled in the "parallel market." At this rate of exchange Argentine goods and services were very cheap. But the long siesta was hard to get used to. Businesses closed at noon and didn't reopen until 4:00 or 5:00. Everybody went home and enjoyed a long, mysterious interval. Some used the time to go windsurfing, as we knew from the colorful sails that zipped across the river in the afternoons. They paid for this mid-day idyll, however, by working late. The restaurants didn't open until 8:00.

We attended a Kafka play where men portrayed apes shouting aggressively at each other, and a dramatization of poetry by Garcia Lorca. Finally the mechanic called. "I've got the motor running, but the cylinder is ovalled," he said. "It will burn oil until you get it repaired." We were glad for this partial success. We preferred the outboard for going downriver because it is compatible with sailing. So we broke the little-tail down into parts and stowed it away, to be reassembled whenever we should travel upriver again.

On October 4 we went to the local *Prefectura Naval* to get a permit to leave Corrientes. A group of neatly-dressed officers began crafting a document. "You'll have to carry a pilot," one informed us. We made faces of disbelief until a superior officer exempted us from this requirement.

"Your certificate of boater's training, please."

"I'm afraid I don't have one," I said. "They don't require them where I live."

"Then how do you avoid collisions?" he asked, dumbfounded.

I couldn't think of a response. Not hitting other boats seemed pretty elementary. They loaded us with dire warning about thieves and storms, but we had concluded that the *Prefectura* exaggerated all dangers to defend their existence. After three hours of carefully not expressing our thoughts we signed their document *in quadruplicate*!

In the following days the *Prefectos* kept close tabs on us. They insisted that we call or radio them at least once daily. If we stopped near one of their offices we had to report ourselves and get new paperwork. They were paranoid mother hens, friendly busybodies.

Listless heat alternated with blustery cold snaps. Headwinds kept us motoring most of the time. The river was a brown sheet with huge islands and adjoining swamps. Innumerable channels added to or subtracted from the torrent, maintaining a complex balance between the river and its surrounding lagoons. Cattle now outnumbered alligators and capybaras; their trails snaked through the riverine woods. Once a passing storm obliged us to douse all sail and start the motor. In the building waves a sheet got tangled in the propeller. We washed up on a sandbank covered with breaking waves. Wading chest-deep in the cold muck we manhandled *Thurston* into the lee of the bank, where we dried our clothes and waited out the gale.

In the city of Paraná another yacht club hosted us. The sailing group invited us to barbecues featuring roasted beef and sausage. Everyone kissed each other on the cheek and was exquisitely polite. Twice a week the five-to-ten-year-olds launched their Optimist prams. They milled about the basin, working their tillers and sheets, until a powerboat tied them together in a long line and towed them upstream so they could race back to the yacht club with assistance from the current. Teenagers sailed Lasers or went wake-boarding.

In Rosario, our biggest Argentine city so far, we ghosted past miles of grain terminals. The ships' homeports included Limassol, Manila, and Monrovia. When we stopped at a marina to ask directions an athletic-looking yachtsman offered to arrange a courtesy mooring for us. It turned out he was also a symphony cellist! Thinking this a good place to make further progress on the Honda, we accepted.

This time we took the motor apart ourselves. We split open the crankcase, marveling that something the size of a lunch box could propel us so far and so fast. We removed the piston and took the cylinder to a specialist. "These are disposable, they can't be fixed," he said. We bought a small torque wrench and reassembled the motor, tightening to specification. We hadn't stopped the oil consumption but now we knew which parts we needed.

Below Rosario we entered the delta of the Rio Paraná. The channels became smaller and more numerous. Vacation homes dotted the banks. People paddled about in canoes and kayaks. The *Prefectos* called us on our cell phone so much we started turning it off at night. One day upon turning it back on we found that we had missed twenty-nine calls. "They're all Pre*fuck*to numbers!" spit Ginny, a great hater of intrusion. The nickname stuck.

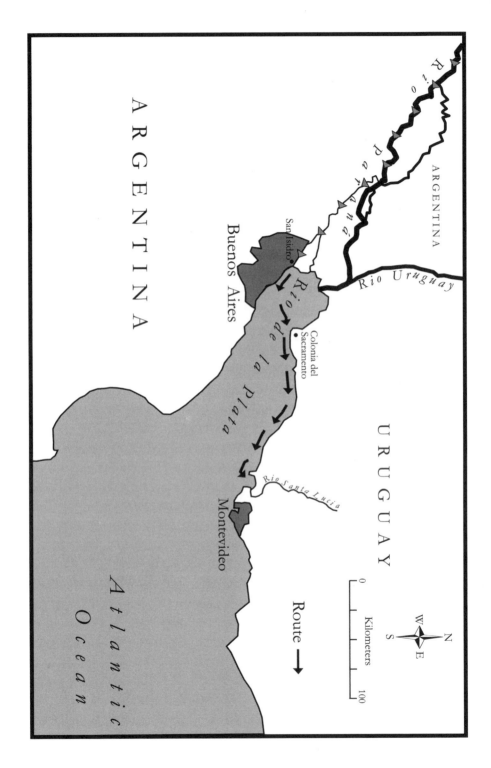

RIO DE LA PLATA:

Chapter 7
THE RIO DE LA PLATA

On October 30 we exited the right-most river mouth and found ourselves in San Isidro, a suburb of Buenos Aires, the skyline of which was visible. These cities are on the Rio de la Plata, called a river because the water is fresh, being the recipient of the rivers Paraná and Uruguay. If it is a river it's the world's widest. But it has no noticeable current and can equally be regarded as a gulf of the Atlantic. Yet another geographical oddity! In any case, there would be no more rivers on which to continue south. It was time to start thinking about the long voyage back home.

The San Isidro waterfront was entirely occupied by yacht clubs, canoe clubs, and rowing clubs. The *Club de Veleros* (sailboats) gave us a courtesy moorage. From here we walked through a posh shopping district to a covered platform thronged with urbanites. When the train came we pressed in and hung onto overhead rails. Forty-five minutes later we arrived at a station of monumental European styling at the northwest edge of downtown Buenos Aires.

It has been said that Argentines are Italians that speak Spanish and think they are French. That many are from Italy is clear from the prevalence of Italian foods and family names. As for francophilia, Citroens, Renaults, and Peugeots dominated the streets, which look Parisian due to their solid flanks of seven-story buildings with mansard roofs and profuse ornamentation. The immense theaters, government *palacios,* and obelisks were all built around the turn of the twentieth century. Argentina then nearly equaled Europe and America in affluence, but this promise faded with the populist totalitarianism of

Juan Peron, the Dirty War of the 1970s (in which leftists battled government death squads), and several monetary collapses. On the Paseo Florida, musicians and tango-dancers performed for tips. In the plaza fronting the President's palace an unkempt band of Falkland Islands War veterans were in their third year of a campout, protesting denied benefits.

We relished the cool nights of the Argentine spring. We learned the quirky buses, trains, and subways. The stamps of twenty countries having filled our passports, we had new pages inserted at the American Embassy. Another ultrasound revealed that our baby was a boy! We sailed to a yacht club in downtown Buenos Aires and savored another week of courtesy mooring in the heart of the metropolis. Two foreign yachts were present, ours and a German sailboat. In their flawless courtesy the club flew the American and German flags from the yardarms of a mast which stood at the foot of a polished brass cannon pointing out to sea.

Ginny's internet research showed that receiving Honda motor parts from the States would be easier in Uruguay, a small country on the north coast of the Rio de la Plata, so we began the excruciating exit procedures. Deadly serious immigration officials detained us in a small, dark room for four hours because of an irregularity in our papers. Finally they conceded that their cohorts on the Paraguayan border had processed our entries incorrectly. It took three trips to the *Prefectura* to get their clearance, and a bus ride to a different part of the city for Customs. But the latter official made up for this bureaucratic indifference by giving us the rare coins we needed for the return bus trip. They cost almost nothing but you couldn't find them! At dawn on November 17, 2012, we motored out of the harbor.

The Rio de la Plata was too wide to see across. The headwind was mild yet the waves were steep. Each time *Thurston* nosed down into a trough the propeller lifted out of the water, revving the engine. Short, steep waves are common in shallow waters such as this. Our Honda's misshapen cylinder still allowed crankcase oil into the combustion chamber, so every two hours we cut the motor and topped up the reservoir. In the afternoon land became visible. The wind changed, allowing us to raise masts and sail into Colonia del Sacramento, a town full of ancient Portuguese ruins and Argentine tourists.

Leaving Buenos Aires

To reach Montevideo, the capital, we would be traveling two hundred kilometers eastward. The coast was a succession of forests and farms, surf-less beaches and low black rocks. Small rivers issued from the land. After leaving Colonia we pulled into one such mouth. We passed a ruined wharf, a quarry, and a path where cattle came down to drink. The encompassing trees were a curious blend of willows, cactus, and palms. We tied to a branch and fell asleep.

"Something's wrong," Ginny mumbled at 4:00 a.m. *Thurston* was sharply down at the bow, and seemed to be on a balancing point; she tipped sideways when we moved. We eased into the cockpit. The tide had dropped. *Thurston's* skeg had caught on a rock that was now thirty inches above water level while the bow floated free. We stabilized her by removing the masts. There was no further remedy in the dark so we went back to sleep.

With it got light I slipped into the dark, chilly water and felt around. We were poised over a scattering of huge, sharp boulders. There was no place to stand and lift. The tide reached its low and starting rising again. The Rio de la Plata's tides are caused less by moon and sun than by the region's mercurial winds, which build the water up on whichever side is to lee. Tide prediction is largely wind prediction. We had no idea what the wind would do next but hoped that the next high would float us off.

On rocks due to tide dropping, Rio de la Plata

Unfortunately, at noon the tide started to drop again. The stern was still two feet high. I hated to pry it off because it would slide down a sharp ridge of rock, but we didn't want to wait another day either. "Okay, let's do this," I said. We inserted a lever between the skeg and rock and lifted. *Thurston* splashed into the water with a cracking sound. The skeg we had installed in Brazil had broken off, the dense wood sinking straight to the bottom. Something else to fix.

As we proceeded east mud gave way to sand. Dunes and pine forests blanketed the shore, reminding us of Washington State's Pacific coast. Reeds grew thick in the estuaries, where little red fishing boats bobbed at their anchors. Leaving *Thurston* in a hidden river bend we walked to a nearby town for groceries, marveling at the clean road-sides and newly-mown pastures, like a Latin American Illinois.

On November 27 we entered the Rio Santa Lucia. On the east bank we found a small yacht club. The facilities were modest but well-tended. The employees were whiskery men who in their spare time tended ducks, dogs, and caged birds. The club members had elected as their "captain" Pancho, a husky retired fisherman who lived aboard an old cruiser. He pulled *Thurston* out on an old trailer so we could build a new skeg, fix deck leaks, and paint the topsides where the gel coat had worn away. He then gave us a courtesy mooring at a dock that the other boats couldn't use because the water was too shallow. The early summer days were long. *Pamperos* (violent southwesters) caused super-high tides. Our dock, which was non-floating, was often underwater, so we used our inflatable kayak to get ashore. Such utility notwithstanding, we sold it before leaving. We had carried it since Honduras but hadn't used it enough to warrant the space it occupied.

When high tides inundated our marina's non-floating docks we used our inflatable to get ashore.

Our yacht club friends owned small boats of modest value, but their enthusiasm was keen. Pancho raced a Star. Tall, skinny Ruso (so called due to Russian ancestry) owned an old wooden sailboat. One weekend Pancho, Ruso, another sailor, and I competed in a club regatta. The wind was strong and the variable currents added a delightful complexity. The Star won easily. I came in second place, much aided by *Thurston's* shallow draft, which allowed me to cut corners where the others would have run aground. The race ended with a cordial barbecue of steaks, ribs, and sausages over a wood fire in the club's picnic shelter, then a weekend cruise up the Rio Santa Lucia, again with four boats participating.

Thurston (rightmost) participates in the club regatta at our marina near Montevideo

It took five minutes to walk from the yacht club to a bus stop, then forty minutes to ride to downtown Montevideo. The Old City stands on a peninsula enclosing a large harbor. Here we found the customs building, where we learned how to get yacht-in-transit status, exempting us from import duty on the package we expected. The Uruguayans were like the Argentines but with a subtle difference, perhaps as Canadians might be compared to Americans. Marijuana was legal but nobody seemed to smoke it. The president, a former revolutionary who had spent twelve years in prison, wore overalls and drove a VW bug. Controversy and crime seemed nonexistent.

We received the items we had purchased on-line and which our true-blue friends Larry and Karen had forwarded via Georgia. With the new cylinder, piston, rings, and valves we rebuilt the Honda 2HP motor. We enjoyed this meticulous work, examining every part. Our tiny engine responded well to our care. We passed Christmas and New Years of 2012 in good spirits.

It was time to decide how to get back home. We'd started the voyage at 29 degrees north of the equator. We were now 35 degrees south of it. Florida lay 4,000 nautical miles north and 1,000 nm west. We yearned to continue east along the Rio de la Plata then sail north up the Atlantic coast. Study showed that the mountainous, island-strewn littoral around São Paulo and Rio de Janeiro would be great for cruising. But the coasts in southern Brazil, which we would encounter first, would be stormy and refuge-less. So we chose to return via rivers. The obvious route was back up the Paraná then along its main stem into Brazil. But that would involve retracing our route to Corrientes, and reacquainting with all those Prefectura control freaks. Instead we decided to ascend the Uruguay River to a point where it and the Paraná almost touch. Then we would get a transport to the Paraná in the vicinity of the Yacyretá dam. We would miss out on the segment of the Paraná between Corrientes and the dam, but smaller rivers are usually more interesting. Also we would have Uruguay on our right much of the way and we were enjoying that country immensely.

The president of the yacht club urged us to stay free of charge until the baby came. A member who was a doctor promised us free medical attention. Our friends' warmth and generosity were very touching, but we couldn't sit still that long, and Ginny preferred that George be Brazilian. So on January 7, 2013, we began sailing west the way we had come. After three years we were homeward bound!

Chapter 8
LET'S HAVE HIM IN BRAZIL

On our first day out the oil seal on our newly-rebuilt outboard leaked, causing the automatic clutch to slip. We pulled into the mouth of the Rio Cufré, carried the motor to a hollow in the dunes, and took it apart again. Our side of the river was wilderness, the other side was a campground full of vacationing families. Tied up next to us on the steep, sandy bank was an Uruguayan sailing couple. Ricardo was a satellite communications technician, Sandra was a high school teacher. They drove us around the rural countryside until we found a new oil seal, and had us over for dinner in their cockpit. We shared an interest in not only boats, but literature. I had been reading *Martin Fierro,* an epic poem written in the 1870s in the style of the Argentine gaucho ballads. Ricardo and Sandra helped me translate the slangy old Spanish. "Even young Uruguayans can't understand this dialect anymore, so much have times changed," they said.

We returned to Colonia, where we had first landed in Uruguay, and continued to the huge, flat islands where the Paraná and Uruguay rivers join to form the Rio de la Plata. For two days the Uruguay was wide, with only tidal currents. Then it shrank until we no longer saw sea horizons and faced a steady stream. We rowed, sailed, and motored in equal proportions, camping in small river mouths among sand flats and weeping willows, dipping in the river to cool off on hot evenings. One of our stops was Villa Soriano, the oldest European settlement in Uruguay. In this small town we found the birthplace of Jose Artigas. His early career was in cattle smuggling. Though of Spanish descent, his sympathies were with the guachos, the cowboys of mixed

Amerindian and Spanish ancestry. When Britain invaded the Rio de la Plata in 1806 he helped fight them off, then became Uruguay's founding father upon independence from Spain. In Montevideo we had seen larger-than-life bronze statues of him on horseback. Here he was life-size, brightly-painted, in gaucho garb with the traditional long knife in a scabbard at the small of his back, sitting on a stump with a humorous expression on his face, next to a dog and a native boy. We felt that this depiction was more in keeping with the humble, homespun nature of his country.

Squeezing through a drainage pipe on a creek we explored in Uruguay

On January 26 we reentered Argentina at the city of Concordia. Here the Salto Grande dam blocks the river, but new friends at the *Club Regatas Concordia* trailered us around it to the reservoir above. Its thick arms extended west into Argentina and east into Uruguay. Continuing north, we cut from point to point, camping in coves. Sometimes we stuck an anchor in the beach, other times we tied to a branch.

LET'S HAVE HIM . . .

Once we tied to a cattle fence sloping down into the water and were visited by a curious herd. As the lake narrowed a current again opposed us. Whoever built the dam had not cut down the trees first. The rising water had killed them, but their tops still stood above river level, obstructing the near shore. In some cases the above-water part had rotted away, leaving a stump just below water level. We often hit these but they were soft, harmless. There were few houses, but we sometimes passed swarthy fishermen standing shoulder-deep in the river, immobile except for their heads, which slowly turned to watch as we passed. This posture kept them cool while allowing them to cast their hooks further into the river. We gave them wide berth to avoid catching their lines in our propeller. Every few days the sluggish heat built into a violent storm, obliging us to tuck into a lily-filled inlet flanked by tall, vine-covered forests. The banks were low, the forests subtropical. There were broad-leafs interspersed with pines, palms, and bamboo, also vast plantations of eucalyptus for making paper pulp. Howler monkeys reappeared.

Howler monkey on the Rio Uruguay

Uruguay gave way to Brazil on the right bank. After a long day of sailing or motoring we welcomed a quiet evening under the southern stars. Yellow and green fireflies flew about us. When we washed our dishes in the river, bending over the gunwale to reach the whirling, semi-transparent water, hordes of minnows fought for the scraps. They also bit us we when bathed, but their tiny jaws never broke our skin.

Our little outboard motor developed a fuel system problem so we pulled into a creek mouth to fix it. "Damn, it's a *Prefectura!*" said Ginny, noting a boat and a little building with a radio antenna on the bank. But the usual hassles did not transpire. A lanky officer, off-duty in shorts and T-shirt, told us how boring the work was. "Nothing happens here except sometimes the Brazilians cross over with contraband fireworks," he said. "For a month at a time we don't see our families." He offered us ice, water, and *mate* tea. We located the problem, a restrictive gas filter, and left in the morning.

A week out from Concordia we reached Santo Tomé, a small city where the Uruguay River passes within a hundred miles of the Paraná. It had a boat ramp and highway access, so here we sought transportation to the larger watercourse, which we would ascend to Foz do Iguaçu. We hoped to arrive there in time to have our son.

A tattooed canoe salesman agreed to tow us there with his canoe carrier for $400. It didn't go well. Upon backing his trailer into the river we found that its side posts were too close together. *"No problema,"* he said. He dashed home, got a grinder, and cut the posts off. He didn't cut them low enough, however. When we loaded *Thurston* again the sharp stubs of the sawn-off posts gouged her sides. Also the axle was too far forward, or the weight too far aft. "The tongue is lifting up," I warned. "There should be positive weight on the trailer hitch!" He ignored me. On the way to his house the hitch lifted off the ball, the car decelerated, and the tongue smashed his trunk in. "My brother-in-law can fix that," he grumbled. I shifted *Thurston's* equipment forward until the tongue weight was positive.

By the time we left it was midnight. This suited our driver because there were fewer highway checkpoints at night and he was in violation of something. Not knowing where we would get put in, I stipulated only that it be in the Paraná River upstream of the Yacyretá

Dam. *"No problema,"* he said. He chain-smoked and drank beer while Ginny and I dozed in the back seat. At 3:30 a.m. he backed us into a body of water with suspiciously strong current for a reservoir. *"No problema,* you're above the dam," he said, and drove off.

Dawn of February 11 revealed, looming above us, the *downstream* face of the huge Yacyretá dam shared by Paraguay and Argentina. He'd probably taken us there to avoid checkpoints. The dam had a lock but we would have to deal with the dreaded *Prefectura Naval.*

We were in a town called Ituzaingó. We found the local *Prefectos* and surrendered ourselves to them. A meeting was convened in the chief's office. Various officers gravely expounded upon the perils of the lock and the reservoir above.

"The Paraguayan smugglers are a menace!"

"Calm weather can quickly change into a killer storm!"

"The waves come at you from all directions at once! And you can't go ashore because of the drowned forests! No boats go there!"

Again we were asked for our certificates of boater training. We had none since no comparable license existed in Washington State. We showed them the *zarpe* in which the Prefectura in Concordia had already authorized us to navigate to Foz do Iguaçu, and some magazines in which our articles had been published. "You can see that we're experienced sailors," we argued.

"I am sorry," said the chief, "Without a boating certificate I cannot permit you to go through the lock. But I have a friend who might give you a ride past the reservoir. Good luck!"

A young officer drove us to the office of a company that gives boat rides. "I have no trouble giving you a ride to Posadas," said the manager, referring to the city at the head of the reservoir. "Just give me some gas money." He hooked a Land Rover to a trailer, loaded us into the car, and drove to the waterfront. The *Prefecto* returned to his office separately. "I didn't want to tell you in front of him, but I can't take you all the way to Posadas," he confided. "I'll take you past the dam, to a ranch on the lake. You'll be OK there." He pulled *Thurston* out of the water and drove us out of town, our second transport in three days.

We rumbled along twenty miles of red dirt roads through pasture and forest, avoiding the highway for the same reason our previous transporter had travelled at night: to avoid inspections. When we got to a cluster of buildings on a big lake he backed the boat down a gentle bank. We untied and climbed aboard. "When you pass *Prefectura* stations stay at least a kilometer from shore so they can't bother you," he advised.

As we motored out into this new reservoir we wondered what so terrified the *Prefectos*. It looked no different from the one we had navigated on the Rio Uruguay. After a couple hours we reached an island consisting of a single huge sand dune, uninhabited and barren. We climbed to the top. Was this a drug-smuggling base? Were we being watched? Paraguay was visible to the north. The "deadly" lake was like a mill pond, hot and airless.

Resuming our transit we stayed far from shore until we had passed what looked like a *Prefectura* station, given its tall tower, then pulled into a cove surrounded by open grazing land and rolling hills. We relaxed in the cockpit as the air cooled and the sky turned purple and red. Doves cooed, cicadas whirred. Ginny cooked vegetarian spaghetti. We had just started eating when a boat approached.

"Dammit, it's *Prefucktos!*" Ginny swore. They pulled alongside, their twin outboards idling. "I'm sorry," they said. "This area is unsafe due to cattle rustlers. We have orders to bring you back to our base."

They tossed us a line. We crammed our meal as they towed us to the station we had passed. The senior officer came out. "The Ituzaingó *Prefectura* is very unhappy with you," he said. "They prohibited you from going out into the lake but you went anyway. You'll have to stay here until I get authorization from Posadas." We turned in bursting with repressed anger. Our little cove had been protected but here the waves made sleep difficult.

In the morning they let us go after a few phone calls. As we continued the reservoir narrowed and a current asserted itself. Posadas was our last Argentine city, capital of the Province of Misiones, named for the Jesuit missions that once controlled this region. Our Google Earth-derived GPS shoreline was inaccurate; it turned out the dam had been raised higher since the satellite image was taken. The old yacht club was now underwater. They had relocated it nearby, but the new one had no jetty or dock. They gave us a buoy to tie to and a canoe to get to shore and back. The water was too rough to sleep aboard so we set up our tent on land.

LET'S HAVE HIM . . .

It was mid-February. Ginny's due date was March 18. We had decided to have our baby in Brazil near the huge waterfall where Argentina, Paraguay, and Brazil come together. I read the midwifery chapter in our *Where There Is No Doctor* book in case Ginny went into labor prematurely. The *Prefectura* continued to plague us in this final stretch. Armed vessels sometimes accompanied us, "For your safety," they said. We camped where they told us, or hid deep in swampy holes where their searchlights couldn't penetrate, squeezing in among trees adapted to seasonal flooding, pushing past floating logs, and tucking under spider-filled branches. Thus ensconced we felt safe, and the Prefectos did not contest these faits accompli.

Butterflies swarmed wherever the sun penetrated to a solid surface, be it *Thurston* or a muddy bank. We had entered a rainy season, or simply a region that has no dry season. The land became hills and tall basalt cliffs. Every few kilometers we passed an indent in the shoreline at the head of which a stream fell off a cliff into the river. Waterfalls peeped out through the forests that blanketed the canyon walls. Occasionally a red dirt road sloped up out of the valley. On the Argentine side the road ends were undeveloped, but on the matching Paraguayan side the steep, diagonal track would be lined with wall-to-wall wooden shops, those on the downhill side perched on tall, precarious stilts over the void. "Argentines go to the other side to buy cheap clothes and shoes," we were told.

The river now flowed through a gorge. In the middle the current spiked to five knots, so we retired the two-horse outboard and mounted the five-horse little-tail. It was too brutish for Ginny to steer for long. We stuck close to the bank to take advantage of the countercurrents in the many coves. The forty-five degree slope was studded with jagged black outcroppings. Those at and just below water level posed hazards. Intent on progress I cut close to the rocks, clipping one now and then. If the bump was hard we felt under the floorboards to make sure we weren't taking on water. The current along the bank splintered into myriad whirls. *Thurston* spun this way and that as we maneuvered from one patch of water to another, squirreling left and right.

We skirted around nets strung from the shore out to an anchor, buoyed by a string of plastic bottles. The Paraguayans, poorer than the Argentines, fished from wooden rowboats. They were rumored to constantly sneak over to the Argentine side for illegal purposes such as tree poaching. Ferrymen rowed passengers across, dropping them off at trails leading up the 500-foot-tall bank. Like us they took advantage of the longshore eddies. They rowed upstream in them to compensate for being swept downstream while crossing over.

Walking to a town for provisions on a hot day, boat in background, Rio Paraná, Argentina

On February 22 we turned right into the Rio Iguazú (Spanish spelling), which entered from the east. Its canyon walls, like those of the Paraná, were heavily forested and too steep to see the cities above: Puerto Iguazu on the Argentina side and Foz do (Mouth of the) Iguaçu on the northern (Brazilian) side. Ciudad del Este, Paraguay, lay on the west bank of the Paraná. Each country had a prominent monument at its corner of the Triple Frontier. Puerto Iguazú was the smallest of the three cities. Its waterfront consisted of a flat spot with some government buildings and a sewage outlet. To get our bearings we walked up a steep road to the town proper. There, busy streets ran at all angles. It was a base for tourists coming to see the Argentine side of the Iguaçu Falls, located ten miles up the Iguaçu.

Ginny's mom, Lois, was scheduled to arrive on March 15th. We hoped to then move into an apartment in Foz. Meanwhile we needed a place to live aboard, so we took a bus across the bridge to Brazil. It turned out that, due to waterfront cliffs, Foz do Iguaçu's only accessible waterfront was directly across the Rio Iguazú from where our boat was tied up. To get there from the Brazilian side we walked a long, angling road down into the canyon. It was merely a small terminal for putting sand ashore. Every day a steel boat went out and sucked up sand from the riverbed, then came back and slurried it up to a dewatering enclosure. From there a front-end loader hefted it onto trucks which carried it away. The terminal included a boat ramp, an office, and a one-man *Policia Federal* post. We didn't exactly get permission to tie up there, but no one objected to our request.

With this encouragement we returned to Argentina and started their exit procedures. The under-worked *Prefectos* now invented a new twist: they called ahead to their Brazilian counterparts to see if they would grant us entry, failing which, presumably, they would not let us go. This was ridiculous on several levels, the first being that no self-respecting bureaucrat would answer a question like that in the abstract, without the person standing in front of them with all their papers. "Someone will get back to you," a nameless Brazilian told a nameless Argentine. But we had a trick up our sleeves. Foreseeing that the *Prefectos* would delay us we had left our clothes at a laundromat a half hour's walk away, on the plateau, so we weren't ready to go yet! By the time our clothes were washed, dried, folded, and put away they had given up on their whimsical inquiry as to how the Brazilians might receive us. They then carefully crafted a flowery new clearance paper, the last in a sheaf of documents that we weren't very sentimental about, but which we appreciated for their sheer absurdity.

We rowed across to the sand terminal, dropped an anchor from the stern, and tied the bow to the steep bank. We then looked into paperwork on that side. Nobody ever arrived by boat so the authorities didn't know what to do. We took buses here and there until someone in an office downtown advised us to go and get our passports stamped at the international bridge. The usual procedures for bringing a boat in simply didn't occur, a laxity which we greatly appreciated.

We paid a deposit at a maternity hospital, then looked for a place for us, Lois, Ginny's sister Carley, and her man Matt to stay from March 14 to April 17. Lois would be paying so we tried to fill her specifications: three bedrooms, kitchen, air conditioning, close to downtown, at a good price. After scouring the city's real estate offices, classified ads, and web sites we concluded that such a place did not exist, but Lois graciously lowered her expectations a bit, allowing us to reserve an apartment in a large complex. Then we settled into the sand terminal for the two weeks that would pass before we could move in.

The tie-up was tricky. There was no dock or buoy. The shore was a steep canyon-side. We needed a perpendicular alignment in order to step ashore at the bow. The stern was over deep water, so that rode had to be run out as far as possible, and even then it could never have the proper scope (length of rode divided by depth of water). What's more, the glossy, red-brown river often rose or fell as much as two meters overnight due to erratic releases from dams up both the Iguaçu and Paraná rivers. In our favor, there wasn't much current and the holding ground was a heavy soil. We made it work by constantly adjusting the bow and stern lines for water level. Hardly anyone was around except on weekends when a few families set up chairs and umbrellas at the foot of the boat ramp and fished as if it were a beach.

Ginny's iron and blood sugar levels were low, and vegetarian foods were scarce, so she had started eating meat. She now slept at the wide end of the cabin by the open hatch. Heat, back pains, and worry kept her awake at night. Our solar-powered electrical system lacked capacity to run our fan very long so we installed a supplemental battery and a fan of lower amperage. A foray into the city began with me snubbing the bow line so she could ease onto the steep, muddy bank. Then we walked two kilometers along a steep road that angled up over the cliff and down into a neighborhood where there was a bus stop, stopping frequently to ease any shooting pains or faintness. We always did a lot of "trudging," but the term was never more apt than during her pregnancy.

Foz do Iguaçu was a city of 250,000, the result of a building boom when the huge Itaipu dam was built. Nearby Iguaçu Falls drew tourists. So did Ciudad del Este, Paraguay, the infamous duty-free zone and smuggling center. Making the most of what Brazil had to offer we ate mangoes and chocolate and drank beer from returnable liter bottles. I also bought a used bicycle for excursions on my own.

On the 15th we picked Lois up at the airport and moved into the apartment. Naturally talkative, Lois was so excited she switched from subject to subject like a hummingbird sniffing flowers. At the apartment she showered us with gifts. Then we sat on the sofa and feasted on pizza and ice cream. The air-conditioning was a blessing.

Four days later Ginny woke up feeling "different somehow." By 8:00 a.m. she was having contractions every four minutes. I called a taxi, but when I tried to open the security gate that controlled access to our wing our key didn't work! We were stuck inside with Ginny in labor! I yelled and kicked at the gate. Finally somebody reached through the bars and made our key work.

The taxi ride took only a few minutes. At the hospital Ginny was laid on a gurney. While Lois and I signed her in, staffers examined her, pronounced her "Ready!," and whisked her away. Seeing she was gone I hurried after, asking directions, taking an elevator down a floor. There I came to a pair of locked doors. They didn't want me in the birthing room! I shouted and banged until someone dressed me in scrubs and let me through.

In the inner sanctum Ginny was screaming, thrashing, literally foaming at the mouth. *"Tranquilo!"* cried the doctor. A brawny nurse passed her arm through the metal bars on either side of the birthing bed, ready to apply force. Theirs was not a gentle method. Whenever Ginny had a contraction the nurse clamped her arm down and levered the bulge vent-ward. "Push!" she yelled. I held Ginny's hand, translated, and cried.

The agony lasted thirty minutes. Then they snipped the cord and showed us our baby, George Iguassu Ladd. He was healthy, calm, and chubby at 8 pounds, 11 ounces.

Chapter 9
UP THE PARANÁ, DOWN THE ARAGUAIA

Southern-hemisphere autumn brought cooler weather. Following our son's birth on March 19th we spent a pleasant month in our rented apartment in Foz do Iguaçu, Brazil. Ginny's sister and her boyfriend stayed with us for a while, then moved on to other adventures. We got George Iguassu Ladd a shiny new Brazilian passport, and on his seventh day took him to the waterfall from which he derives his middle name. A mile and a half wide and 270 feet tall, it dwarfs Niagara Falls and spews a mist that swirls high over the canyon. I held George up in the eddying droplets with the falls in the background. He looked good up there, in tune with all that primordial freshness.

When Ginny's mother flew home we found a trailer and got *Thurston* transported from the sand terminal to the Lake Itaipu Yacht Club, on the huge reservoir north of the city, above Itaipu Dam. We parked her under a tree and rearranged the cabin. George now slept beside Ginny up forward. I made a new sail cover and new hatches for the aft stowage compartment, the store-bought ones having always leaked. Yacht club employees in matching blue T-shirts kept the grounds immaculate while tufted capuchin monkeys feasted on soursops in a tree behind the restaurant. During meals I studied Brazilian language and history.

On May 30 we started rowing and motoring up the lake, which is an impoundment of the Paraná River. Paraguay was to our left, Brazil to our right. The reservoir was an inland sea with wooded shores. Sportsmen fly-fished from aluminum skiffs. Fishermen in planked boats tended nets. We applied life jacket, ear-protectors, sunglasses, and

Back underway with a new crewmember

sunscreen to George as necessary. We had chosen cotton diapers to avoid garbage, but keeping up with the laundry was tough. Ginny scrubbed them in the river then I hung them on a line running from the mainmast to a pole at the stern. The line had room for fifteen articles. Fortunately, winter in central Brazil is extremely dry. On big days we filled and emptied the clothes line three times! Sailing and clothes-drying were incompatible, so we missed out on some good winds.

At Guaíra, a town at the head of the reservoir, we paddled up a creek until we came to a ramshackle boat shed sheltering fifteen long, slender dories with inboard engines. The owners were a fishermen's cooperative. At their invitation we squeezed in with them, appreciating the roof over our heads. They and their families lived in small homes along an adjoining street. They had us over for meals and took us on errands in their rattly cars. Little girls brought us Ramen noodle packages, and candy and toys for George. We were told, for the umpteenth time, of someone who several years before had kayaked down the river. Like that half-forgotten adventurer, we were newsworthy.

Fishermen families welcome us under their boat shed, Guaíra, Brazil

Leaving Guaíra we were in current again. We ran the long-tail motor slow, averaging seven kilometers per hour. Both banks were now in Brazil, so the naval patrols dropped off. George appreciated frequent stops, so we often strolled sandy banks and forest trails. It took two and a half days to pass Ilha Grande, our longest river island to date at 130 kilometers. With the river undivided again it was three kilometers wide, gargantuan considering how far upstream we were. Corn blanketed the rolling hills, dotted with neat little towns, cleft with deep valleys.

By June 10 the water had became crystal clear because we were approaching another dam (the silt settles out in the reservoirs). The Sergio Matto dam has a lock but the local fishermen weren't allowed to use it. To differentiate ourselves we hoisted our masts and flags. Stopping within sight of the lock we hailed on Channel 16. Someone took our data and said to approach. The operator was a tiny figure in a glass structure high over the downstream gate, which now lifted. We paddled into the chamber, big enough for a hundred *Thurstons,* and tied to a floating bollard in a vertical track. Creaks and groans echoed all around, then the water began swirling. We rose twenty meters, then the upstream gate opened. It was dark when we emerged into this new reservoir, but we soon found a sandy cove in which to anchor.

The next day, my 60th birthday, we relaxed in brilliant sun and waded in the cool, shallow water. The following nights we camped in a series of achingly lovely coves. They were generally creek mouths, marshy at their heads, with forested banks and rising farmland beyond. We saw capybaras, otters, parrots, macaws, and tapir tracks five inches across! Alas, we never saw the tapirs themselves.

On June 14 we reached Presidente Epitácio, a small city on the east bank. We pulled into a lily-lined inlet and nosed up to a bank among some recreational boats. The land was park-like, gently rising. To our left a couple of steel boats were getting welded up. To our right was a small open-air restaurant.

In Presidente Epitácio before leaving for São Paulo. Notice tippiness of boat.

As usual people took an interest in us. Reporters arrived. The marina manager invited us to stay in a guest house. Downtown was a ten-minute walk away. It was a good place to leave *Thurston* while we went to the U.S. consulate in São Paulo to get George an American passport. So we lined up a Couch Surfing host and caught the 8:00 p.m. bus.

Dawn found us in a terminal extending several stories underground. There we caught a subway to the city's core. Fascinated with its history, we found the old Jesuit school where mass was first held in 1554. São Paulo was Brazil's first inland settlement, seventy kilometers from the coast and 2,600 feet above sea level, therefore cool. It grew as the jumping-off point for the *bandeirante* explorations, wherein hardy Portuguese canoed the rivers for years on end in search of gold and Indian slaves. They always carried aloft the Portuguese flag, or *bandeira,* hence the name. Another new type of man, the *gaúcho,* ranged southward, adapting the plains to cattle herding. For centuries everyone spoke a lingua franca based on Guarani. In Paraguay Guarani is still the everyday language, but in Brazil so many Europeans immigrated that Portuguese took over. Now São Paulo, population twenty-two million, is the biggest city in the Southern Hemisphere. We obtained a 445-page atlas that prided itself on depicting all 131,249 streets! It is a metropolis of many centers, each a cluster of skyscrapers.

We found our amiable hosts, Vinicius and Fernanda, in a common-wall house in a hilly sub-city called Butantá. They and two roommates were all recent graduates of the University of São Paulo engineering school. They gave us a spare bedroom, keys to the door, and bicycles to use. Our hosts were leftists, active in the anti-corruption demonstrations then shaking the country. We got the passport process started, toured museums, and generally explored the metropolis using complex subway, rail, and bus systems. Whatever the conveyance, everyone cooed at George. Men and women of all ages tossed phrases like, *"Ay, que pequeninho fão bonitinho e branquinho!"* ("My what a lovely little boy, so cute and white-skinned!") George smiled ecstatically in response to each show of attention.

With time to kill pending the arrival of George's passport, we got another Couch Surfing date, this time in Ouro Preto (Black Gold) in the mountainous state of Minas Gerais (General Mines). In 1696, a hundred and fifty years before the California Gold Rush, *bandeirantes* found gold in these steep hills and creeks. Wealth-seekers rushed from São Paulo and Rio de Janeiro into what was then a wilderness. They were nobles and commoners, Europeans and creoles, masters with slaves. The newly rich built a city of steep cobblestone streets and two-story townhouses. The times were still medieval. They built little alters like false balconies into their homes' exterior walls so that saints would protect them. They flooded the town with baroque and rococo churches. All this still stands. The churches are packed with primitive but colorful paintings, wooden statuary, carved soapstone, and gold-leaf. The most famous architect and sculptor, Aleijadinho (Little Cripple), was a leper who completed his final works with prosthetics attached to his limbs because he no longer had hands. Our hosts were a young couple who spent their days trying to sell illustrated poetry in the streets. Their only furniture were mats and wooden crates they had found on the street after market day. We stayed with them three days in a rental house on top of a hill so tall that it was usually in the clouds, cold and misty.

We also took a bus to Rio de Janeiro, Brazil's most beautiful city and for a long time its capital. Set among sugarloaf mountains, scalloped bays, and luxurious beaches, it rises from a commodious harbor to steep urbanized hillsides. Visiting these places helped us understand how Brazil came to be. When Napoleon occupied Portugal in 1808, King João of Portugal moved his court to Rio. When he returned to Portugal his son remained to rule an independent Brazil. Various separatist movements were crushed, preserving Brazil as a single entity while Spain's New World empire crumbled into eighteen separate countries, all relatively weak. This allowed Brazil to win the race for the interior of the continent. Portuguese-speaking settlers spread out in the footsteps of the *bandeirantes*, protected by soldiers. Our host at this final stop was a friend of Vinicius. We stayed at his condo near the beach. Our favorite discovery in Rio was the Real Gabinete Portuguese de Leitura (Royal Portuguese Reading Library). It was a gem of arches and spires consisting of little more than a three-story atrium filled with antique books, a sort of Gothic altar to the beautifully soft language of Portugal.

Back at Vinicius' place in São Paulo we celebrated our third wedding anniversary. Our friends Francisco and Berlane, from Manaus, were in town so we got together for a trip to Santos, the port city nearest São Paulo. Then George's passport came. Our parting memory of São Paulo is of kites. Kids flew them everywhere. If there was no park they flew them in the street, struggling to get their little squares of paper and balsa up through a gap in the cables and power lines. Once the kite was up the boy had to stay put, but his kite was free to fly around with the wind.

These side trips were fun and informative but the voyage itself was our passion, so we gladly returned to the Paraná River on July 11. At Presidente Epitácio it is impounded by a dam so there was no current to fight. We ran the Honda 2HP slow and cruised for four hours on one liter of gas. We cut across the lake's huge arms, navigating from point to point, threading through forests of dead standing trees. Weekend boaters idly fished under colorful umbrellas. The landscapes were open and watery, full of greenery and wildlife. We camped behind low islands, luxuriating in the quietude. The southern constellations shone brightly in the dark sky.

The many dams on the middle and upper Paraná facilitate upstream travel because still water is easier than contrary current. But each dam was an unknown. We never discovered a way to research them in advance. The next one, the Jupiá, locked us through. The one after that, the Ilha Solteira, didn't have a lock, but Vinicius had a friend there named Vicente. This Good Samaritan quickly got a truck and trailer together and pulled us out at a boat ramp. Ginny and George were seated in the cockpit and I was crouched on the foredeck. We expected him to stop and rearrange us once we were out of the water, but evidently he saw nothing odd in proceeding as we were. He just kept going and we all carefully stayed put, the wind in our hair, as he drove eight kilometers to the ramp above the dam! We had surmounted the sixth of seven dams on this ascent. Only one more to go!

Our six-month visas would soon run out and we were still in the middle of this immense country. We would have to leave *Thurston* and fly out, so we found a cyber café and bought tickets to exit via Goiânia, the capital of Goias State. It was near our route, on the heights separating the Paraná and Amazon basins.

Lock at Jupiá Dam, Rio Paraná

A cold front hit. The southerlies were too violent to sail with George aboard so we rowed, the waves pitching *Thurston* as they passed under. The rolling hills reminded me of the big Missouri River reservoirs in Montana and the Dakotas but with greener grass. Flying clouds blocked the sun until it reached the horizon, where it peaked through a slit, firing to gold the palm trees dotting the pastures. As we veered left into a bay the waves diminished. We then steered into the full protection of a hook-shaped spit made of pebbles the color of peanut skins. Eager to walk we stepped onto the crinkly gravel. Beyond a narrow belt of woods stretched pasture of low, soft curvature. We hiked cow paths, at one point almost stepping on a big armadillo. A flock of emus, the South American ostrich, hopped out of our way. Tapering waterways split the land here and there as the bay subdivided and stabbed into the land. The only sounds were of wind, waves, and birds.

On July 24 the Paraná split into its two sources, the Paranaiba and the Grande. We continued up the former. The days were hot and sunny, the nights cold and dewy. A new kind of no-see-um appeared, with clear, butterfly-like wings. One evening, as we relaxed by a brushy bank, a giant anteater strolled past, like the one we saw on the Orinoco.

At São Simão Dam the president of the local fishermen's union trailered us to our final reservoir. Two days later we turned left up the Rio Dos Bois (River of the Cows). Tired of rowing, I turned the sliding seat over to Ginny. Per usual I said "Port!" or "Starboard!" until she came on course, then said "Mark!" so she could row directly away from the landmark of her choice. But she kept drifting off. "Port! Watch your mark!" I said.

"I was using a cow!" Ginny laughed. "I guess they move too much." She went back to using hills or trees, and we stayed on course.

On August 2 we turned left (northwest) onto the Rio Verdão. We soon hit our first rapid. It was shallow and gravelly, so we got out and pulled *Thurston* through. At the next rapid we switched to the 5.5 HP little-tail motor. This increased our power and reduced our draft because its propeller didn't immerse so much. Even so we barely made it, I poling with a bamboo staff while Ginny wrestled the little-tail's long tiller. The rapids slowed our progress.

We had been studying the upcoming portage off-and-on since Manaus, when we decided to hop over into the Paraná basin. The transport from the north-flowing Guaporé to the south-flowing Paraguay had gone well. Now we were a thousand kilometers east of that portage, ready to jump from a different tributary of the Paraná to a different tributary of the Amazon. As for the latter, the 2,000-kilometer-long Araguaia was the logical choice. We could launch in the city of Barra do Garças.

The best place to pull ourselves out was less clear. The Verdão went in the right direction, but we didn't know how high we could navigate nor how tall the banks would be. There are no big cities on the Verdão, therefore fewer transport options. Only one town touches it, Maurilândia. Would we reach it?

The river was a hundred and fifty meters wide, lined with fist-sized stones, rarely more than waist-deep. Rocks protruded here and there. We swerved left and right looking for at least a foot of depth. Rapids became more frequent. With a sharp stern (no planing surface) and nineteen feet of waterline length *Thurston's* maximum hull speed is 5.9 knots. "We're not going to make this one," I kept thinking, but we kept creeping along, motor wide open, our GPS registering one or two kilometers per hour. We reached the critical spot, where the cold water bubbled over a shallow ledge, swirling white around the black rocks. *Thurston's* bow would lift perceptibly and the GPS would go down to zero. Then we would shift a little to left or right, find a slower eddy, and inch through. Eight kilometers before Maurilândia we stopped for the night at an island.

The next day, August 3, the river was even faster. We hit a rock so hard that two floorboards clanged together, pinching Ginny's toe! Each rapid had only one possible route. But the banks were low so one way or another we would be able to get *Thurston* out of the water and onto the road network.

At 11:00 a.m. we approached the town's only bridge. Under it was the fastest rapid yet. Ginny went ashore to photograph the attempt. Too fast! No matter. Seven months after leaving the Rio de la Plata we had ascended to our head of navigation.

Head of navigation on the Rio Verdão. Maurilândia is to the upper right.

Maurilândia was on the west bank, but we were invited to sojourn at a homestead on the east bank. It was a couple acres of bare red earth, well-scratched by chickens. Here the Nortense clan occupied several houses. Our main host, Aldin, ran a sand dredger. His nephew drove a sugar cane truck on the supremely dusty roads around Maurilândia. Everyone fell in love with George. They offered to store *Thurston* for us while we flew back to the States.

My hosts and I scrounged a chain-fall and some rollers. We pulled *Thurston* up under a mango tree, beyond the rainy-season high water mark. We found a hole in the bow below the waterline, from one of those rocks we'd hit. It hadn't leaked because the hull there was backed up by pour-in-place foam. We would repair it when we got back. That had to be at least six months hence because tourists must stay away that long before Brazil allows them back in.

We took a bus to Goiânia where on August 22nd we caught a flight to Atlanta, Georgia. Our sole souvenir was George, our genuine Brazilian Wiggle Monster.

The mandatory suspension of our voyage disturbed our focus the way a phone call might irritate someone doing yoga, but at least our sojourn back in the States allowed us to attend to many pressing matters, including preparations for the next phase. When the six months had ticked past, on February 26, 2014, we found ourselves again in the farming town of Maurilândia. It was now the rainy season, and the dust had turned to mud. We patched the hole in *Thurston's* bottom and installed a new mount that would allow us to adjust the height of our outboard motor. We wouldn't be travelling upriver anymore, so we gave the little-tail motor to our hosts. Then we wandered around introducing ourselves to truck drivers for the 440-kilometer transport to the Araguaia River. This would be one of our longest.

We finally struck a $500 deal with Marcus, the owner of a truck with a tall box in back. His usual line was hauling produce. Five men and three boys got *Thurston* inside, then we drove northwest. Rolling farmland gave way to hills and escarpments. We crossed into the Amazon basin and stopped where the Rio Garças empties into the Rio Araguaia. The town here, Barra do Garças, translates to Mouth of the River of Herons. When we ascended the Guaporé River in 2012 we had traveled southward along the west edge of Mato Grosso State.

Now we would travel northward along its east boundary while descending the Araguaia River.

Arriving at nightfall, we found a boat ramp. It was paved and of good slope, yet Marcus hesitated. He checked his brakes, concerned that air was leaking from them. Gathering his nerve, but not his wits, he backed down until his rear wheels were underwater and the rear of the box was kissing the river. So far so good; we could simply open the double doors and slide *Thurston* out. Then he started pumping the brake and yelling something that sounded like the word for "Pants!" The truck was slipping backward! We hustled out, Ginny with George in her arms. I frantically looked for a stone to stick under a wheel. It was hopeless. Within seconds the truck was well into the fast-flowing river. The water pushing against the box quickly rotated the truck ninety degrees, parallel to shore. It rolled or floated backward until it came up against an underwater obstacle, then stopped. It was twenty-five feet from shore. The river was about 250 yards wide and running swiftly. The slope toward the center of the river was pretty steep. The cab was underwater except the upper six inches. The box was half-submerged. Marcus swam out from an open window. Now I realized that when he had shouted what sounded like the Portuguese for "pants" it was actually a similar-sounding word meaning "chock!" There was no time to appreciate this funniness. The truck could be carried away at any moment.

Starting a bit upstream to compensate for the current I jumped in and swam to the back doors. The river was a thick, reddish brown. It gushed violently around the truck but left a calm eddy at the back. Opening the double doors I found *Thurston* floating calmly inside. Holding onto a bow line I swam her to shore much as one would lead a horse from a burning barn. Someone tied her to a post for me. I grabbed the masts and booms as they floated away. The leeboards and aluminum floorboards, being heavier than water, hadn't escaped. I retrieved them later. Then I swam to the driver's door. Groping through his window I found our daypacks afloat, pressed up against the roof of the cab. They contained a camera, a Sony Walkman, and a Kindle, all ruined, and our documents, which would require careful drying. Everything else we had stowed aboard *Thurston*. We hadn't lost much!

The "port," as they called the area around the boat ramp, had tall concrete steps going down into the water, like a grandstand. It soon filled with soldiers, firemen, news media, and hundreds of onlookers. A pair of scuba divers suited up. They worked with agonizing slowness, but eventually they attached one cable to the front of the truck and another to the side facing shore. Then two massive tow trucks slowly winched in the cables.

By 2:00 a.m. the truck was back on land and the crowd had dispersed. I paid Marcus his money. He had lost control because his hand brake didn't work, the road brakes were bad, and his transmission had gotten stuck in neutral. Normally boastful, he was wretched. "My mouth is dry with shame," he breathed. He had no insurance.

In the morning we recuperated. *Thurston* lay downstream of the steps against a grassy bank. Jet skis zipped around in front of the "grandstand." They spun in tight circles and shot up mountains of foam. One guy rode his machine facing backwards. Another guy had a "matador" routine: while pirouetting his machine he stood with both feet on the floorboard to the inside of his curve, worked the throttle with one hand, and with the other gestured gracefully in the air like he was flagging a bull. The jet skiers never ventured far from the grandstand. Their wakes annoyed us, but the crowd appreciated having something to watch. When night fell the nearby streets became even more jammed. People drank beer in the parks and open-air restaurants while musicians performed beautiful folk ballads.

After provisioning we attempted an upstream excursion to verify that everything was functioning properly. Our two-horsepower outboard motor had been fine the last time we used it, but now its automatic clutch slipped, so we returned to the port. Lazaro, the owner of the outdoor restaurant above the grandstand, took me and the tiny machine to a backyard mechanic on the other side of the Araguaia River. When we took it apart we found that the clutch was full of engine oil. We replaced an oil seal and tried her again. This time she ran rough and lubricant gushed out through the crankcase vent. Opening the engine we found that the clip holding one end of the piston's wrist pin had come loose. The wrist pin had drifted into contact with the cylinder skirt and worn a groove. For the second time we needed a new cylinder and piston.

Buying the parts on the internet was easy. The problem was getting them shipped to us in a timely manner, clearing customs along the way. To double our odds, and end up with a spare set, we bought a cylinder and piston from one outfit and the same parts from another, and had them shipped to different addresses in different states. The latter was easy because the river separated two states. The shipping and import duties would be expensive but we needed to get *Thurston* downriver before dropping water levels exposed sand bars and rocks in key locations.

The river went down as the rainy season tapered off. The days were scorching hot. We climbed a mountain on the outskirts of town and hiked to a distant hot spring and waterfall. For George's first birthday newfound friends gave him a party. To ease our stay the owners of a local ice cream factory installed us in an under-utilized vehicle compound with bedroom, bath, and kitchen. I had an unpleasant experience in a restaurant, however, when I bit into what looked like a stewed potato. It was firmer that I expected so I bit harder. Suddenly my teeth broke into a soft interior and dozens of tiny spines became lodged in my tongue and the walls of my mouth! Our waiter rushed over. "But that is a *pequi*," he said. "You are only supposed to eat the outer flesh!" For an hour Ginny removed spines with a pair of tweezers but she couldn't get them all. I went to a dental surgeon to get the last few out.

One day, on a trip back to the boat, I noticed rodent scat and chew marks. We moved all our stuff to the beach until, with no place left to hide, a rat broke cover. He scrambled about until I killed him with a bamboo pole. He had torn holes in our packaged food and minced various bags and clothing.

We cleaned this mess up, but our rodent visitations weren't over. The next one, upon being chased about, squeezed into a crevice in the nearly inaccessible area under the cockpit. To counter this maneuver we had no choice but to gather some rags, then lay awake in our bunk that night until we heard him chewing things outside his refuge. On an agreed signal we sprang into action! I harried him, allowing Ginny to reach his hiding place before he could get there. Squirming into place she jammed rags into the crack. We now treated him like the first rat: we started removing things. When he went for his refuge he found no escape from my probing stick. When the boat was nearly empty he materialized from nowhere. The prober was too long to swing, so I grabbed him with my bare hands and smashed his head onto the floor. He died instantly. I hadn't meant to run the risk of being bitten, but a rat aboard a boat is intolerable! We resolved never again to leave them a place to hide.

In Barra do Garças, Brazil. We have leaned our floorboards against the giant steps to facilitate cleaning the boat.

George deserves some space in this narrative so here is a day in his life. He wakes us up at 6:30 a.m. jabbering and crawling all over us with a big, droolly grin. We play games for a while, then he paws through the fruit and veggie department taking a bite out of each item. He smashes his breakfast around his face and onto our clothes. Then a nap, then a bath, then we take him up to the park. He crawls around collecting dirt and new friends. When he sees someone smiling at him he stretches out his arms and says, "Ooooh!" They come over. George and the new friend coo at each other. They invite us to lunch at their house. George meets their pets. When it cools off we go for a walk,

George in a pouch on my back. He is well known so people often stop to talk. Around 8 p.m. we put him to bed. He conks out, spreading his limbs so as to take up lots of space, but we're so exhausted we settle for whatever room is left. In short, he seemed happy.

On April 8 one of the packages finally arrived! Overjoyed, we returned to our mechanic. He had only simple tools but was wonderfully wise and kind. I loved working with him, learning from him. The cylinder had factory defects so he sent me to a machine shop. Neither the machinist nor my mechanic accepted any money. With the motor running again we finally cast off on April 12th.

The tall hills soon melted away leaving only low, green banks. Nobody lived along the river. If we managed to squeeze through the matted riverine brush we found only twisted trees, tall grass, and palm shrubs with thorns like six-inch needles. The river grew with the addition of new tributaries. Because the latter were relatively clear the Araguaia, originally a soupy orange, became clearer until visibility reached one foot. Every morning the temperature quickly rose into the nineties. Ginny and George developed itchy heat rashes. The cockpit was okay with the awning up and the artificial breeze of the moving boat, but the cabin was unbearable because the varnished cedar of our cabin top absorbed heat. We stopped in a small town and painted it white. We frequently doused ourselves and George with the bailer bucket. Dinner became problematic because our white gas stove kept going out. This wasn't surprising since we hadn't seen white gas for two years. We had tried various auto fuels, even aviation fuel, but problems inevitably developed. At night the cabin was too hot for all three of us, so I slept curled up in the cockpit footwell, a space about two feet wide by four feet long.

By day a type of midge caused swollen bites if we stopped at a beach. Mosquitoes necessitated nets at night. Even non-biting insects were a nuisance. At night our headlamps attracted beetles and flies small enough to get through our nets and tickle our faces. Crickets flew aboard, crawled under nets, and pestered us. They all died during the night and required mopping up in the morning.

We saw toucans, roseate spoonbills, and *tuiuius,* the big white stork with a red neck. Black birds gobbled like turkeys, or roosted together in trees, whirring like cicadas. We reacquainted with our old friends the hoatzin and the caracara which, not knowing their true names, we called the Venezuelan Mohawk-Hairdo Chicken and the Paraguayan Eagle.

Each morning I rowed a couple hours. It was good to feel tone in my arms and shoulders again. Every couple days we passed a town with a hotel or two for visiting sports fishermen. Here we got out and stretched our legs, walking George between us, each holding one of his hands. The towns were small and neat with buildings of stuccoed brick. Their river-fronts had sea walls of mortared stone and plazas overlooking the river. We made a point of walking to the edge of town where a road receded across the plain or swamp, connecting that settlement to the rest of the world. Then we walked back to the boat, stopping for a 600 ml bottle of Skol beer on the way. With any luck the bakery might have bread rolls and the vegetable store might have some mangos or carrots.

When evening came we followed still channels into offshoot lagoons and anchored out in the middle to lessen the mosquitoes. We also tied to brush where islands were about to emerge. On one such sunset, far from any real land, we waded in some shallows. The coarse sand gave way until one was buried up to one's ankles, but no further. Suddenly a flash of silver brushed against my ankle. I had bumped into a freshwater stingray but its spiny tail had failed to penetrate my skin. Stingray wounds are notoriously painful.

As we traveled downriver the land grew ever swampier. The surrounding land was a maze of channels and lagoons studded with gnarly old snags. Pink dolphins often followed us. Otters snorted and tumbled in the water. Howler monkeys raised their cacophonous din, unseen in the forest.

We ran the motor at three-sixteenths throttle, sipping gas at one third liter per hour. The awning provided life-saving shade, but it also constricted our forward vision to a small gap between it and the cabin top. We often peeled the awning back to see better. Headwinds pestered us. Ginny had probably spent a hundred hours on Google Earth building our GPS map for the Araguaia due to its countless islands and channels. Her map was reasonably accurate except that the imagery was shot during low water. The river being bigger now, we often navigated where it showed land.

On the Araguaia River

Traveling downriver was so sweet! The scenery changed quickly and rowing was easy. The water convulsed beneath us, spinning us gently left or right. When we sank our oars in the water and pulled, one or the other of them was likely to meet with no resistance, throwing us momentarily off balance. The cause was unevenness of current, upsurges and swirls which etched the river's surface. A ripple line marked the downstream end of each sandbar; if we made it to that line without hitting bottom we would be back in deep water. Whirlpools and upsurges indicated irregularities in the river floor. This was evident when we explored recently emerged islands: dunes and clumps of vegetation had scour troughs downstream of them, allowing us to visualize the eddies. On a larger scale, it was not always clear which way currents were flowing. If we didn't know which way to go around an island we just aimed at it, kept that heading, then let the current sweep us to one side or the other. We were always lining up objects at varying distances and observing how they diverged. Sometimes puffs of river foam moving or not moving relative to a bank told us what we needed to know.

On April 30 we reached São Felix, Mato Grosso. Our second package had arrived in Barra do Garças, so we waited four days while a friend shipped it to us. São Felix is the seat of the Carajás, a major tribe. Every other person on the street was Carajás. They generally wore tattoos, the women with geometric bands around their calves, the men with crude circles around their cheekbones. We befriended a native with a spotted leopard tattooed down his arm. "We used to grow manioc and maize on the emerging islands, but now the government gives us these," he said indicating some food bundles. "I will take them to my village in my canoe." He described how they greet the sun when it rises and say good-bye when it sets, and how they address the river. But if he could be considered a Third World person, he was also First World. He was a biologist, and a cultural exchange program had once sent him on a visit to the Arapaho tribe in Wyoming. "The Carajás and Arapaho are very similar!" he averred.

We started seeing hills again as the state of Goias gave way to Tocantins on the right bank while Mato Grosso State turned into Pará State on the left. The river was now a mile wide. Planked canoes with little-tail motors passed by. The dry season was approaching but we still experienced fierce storms of wind and rain, thunder and lightning. The tempests always came from the east, so we camped on the east bank, where the waves would have no fetch.

The land became higher, less swampy. Tall, wispy palm trees appeared. Dense emergent brush grew along the shores, making it difficult to reach land. We travelled fast to reach the Xambioá rapids (the "X" is pronounced "Sh") before the low-water season, passing so many towns they blurred in our memories. It didn't help that many had similar names, like Aragarças, Aruaná, Araguacema, and Araguaná. Now the houses had vertical plank siding and thatched roofs. The waterfronts often had rustic shelters, half underwater, where beer and snacks would be served when their summer arrived. The locals spoke eagerly of the crowds that would then flock to their beaches, reviving the economy.

Rocks that later might have been a problem were still covered. We hoped that we could also transit the serious rapids that commence at Xambioá, but upon arrival in this lovely town on the Tocantins side we learned otherwise. The local boatmen, who ferry people to a sister city across the river, decided that it wouldn't be safe even to tow us through. Just downstream was a rapid whose roar was audible from town. Rapids continued intermittently for sixty kilometers. Too many rocks were now exposed, and *Thurston's* motor would be insufficient for the turbulence.

Fortunately, across the street there lived a man with a long flatbed truck. His price was reasonable, so we reconvened at a nearby ramp, where many hands helped load *Thurston*, and we were off on our twelfth transport.

Our route took us along seventy kilometers of paved highway then fifty kilometers of rough dirt road. We passed through rangeland and forest, arriving finally at a riverside hamlet called Antonina. It consisted of ten humble houses and an open store/bar. Ferry employees, an agricultural inspector, and a local teenager helped us lower *Thurston* into the water.

Unloading Thurston at the ferry crossing below Xambioá rapids

The opposite bank, which lay in the state of Pará, was a low forest. The only sign of man was a dirt road coming down to the water. Usually the ferrymen had no business. Antonina being more comfortable, they took their leisure on our side. Now and then a vehicle would arrive. Those arriving on the Antonina side would drive onto the barge. Those on the far bank would honk their horn. Either way, the skipper and a deck hand would then saunter down to the landing and fire up their diesel-powered rig. It consisted of a tugboat and barge connected by a pivot. On the tugboat the pivot was on the bow. On the barge it was at the middle of its downstream side. With their screw turning the skipper pushed the rudder hard over. This caused the tug to rotate 180 degrees while the barge remained stationary. Then they chugged across, the tug angling a bit upstream to hold the barge in line. On the far side the deck hand pushed out wheel ramps. The vehicle drove aboard. Then they flipped the tug around again and returned. We observed several iterations of this while putting *Thurston* back together. When the sun went down we drank beers at a dimly-lit patio overlooking the river. George, playing with local kids, walked ninety-three steps, his record to date! Two men tinkered with a little-tail motor.

In the Araguaia's final two hundred kilometers we passed through long stretches where brush and barely-submerged rocks pocked the river's surface. There was no main channel, just a vast sheet of greenish-brown water filtering through a sieve of rough bedrock. We picked our route, slipping over ledges, swirling as the water sucked and surged.

On May 21 we reached the juncture of the Araguaia and Tocantins rivers. Though the Tocantins is the smaller of the two, its name applies to the combined stream, so we had finished with the Araguaia, and with the rapids. The first city on the Tocantins was Marabá, on the left bank. After passing some wooden boats being caulked we tied up at a floating dock overcrowed with vessels. We then ascended a stairway to the top of a tall seawall with a broad view of the river. The vessels competing for room on the dock were open but roofed for shade. All were carrying people to a "party beach" on a sandbar way out in the river. We could barely make out the line of colorful tents there, but the party music easily reached us because sound carries well over water.

The dock was haphazard and undersized. The boats jostled each other to get their bows near the stairway. They squeezed together, wedging their sharp prows forcefully in. When the full complement of passengers had clambered aboard the skipper shoved his boat backwards to escape from the jam. Then he stood on the stern deck, pushed his tiller over, and yanked on a throttle string. "Brraammm!" the engine roared. The boat angled away, his passengers jabbering gaily, his engine belching black smoke.

After a week's layover we recommenced our descent. We weren't in a hurry, yet we rarely stopped because the shore was generally devoid of shade. Nor were there trails for walking. It was more comfortable to keep underway and enjoy the breeze caused by our own motion. Our tarp was like a tunnel. In addition to providing shade it allowed air to flow through.

By the time we reached the reservoir of the Tucuruí Dam the landscape had morphed yet again. The water was like that of the Rio Negro: translucent black and devoid of mosquitoes. Hundreds of tall islands dotted the lake, but they were generally inaccessible. This was due to natural hedges composed of a plant reminiscent of an eight-foot-tall asparagus which grew densely on the banks and on the immersed foreshore. No one had cut the trees when the dam was built, so we weaved through dead trees and tied to them at night.

Our best campsite was on a small island where someone had cleared just enough to step ashore. Inside the perimeter vegetation the rainforest was virgin and relatively open, the trees tall and large-leafed. We hiked to the top of the island, trudging through deep forest litter. The tree cover was too dense for views, but it was good to reacquaint with the rich, clean smells of the Amazonian forest.

After three days travelling north on the lake we reached 75-meter-tall Tucuruí Dam. They wouldn't lock us through, so we found a cheap transport to a ramp below. The common launch now was a wooden boat twenty to thirty feet long with a diesel engine, a steering station in the blunt bow, and a stern so long and tapering that no weight could be carried aft of amidships. These streamlined vessels were gracefully fitted with a variety of roofs and cabins, and their paint jobs were often quite beautiful.

We stayed on a deserted beach below the dam for a few days. All around was empty forest. The river dropped nine feet at night and rose again each morning, perhaps due to a diurnal pattern in how water was released through the hydroelectric plant. To avoid drying out while we slept I tied *Thurston* to a branch overhanging deep water. In the morning I climbed the tree and retrieved our line so we could move over to the beach. Then we learned to loop the line over the branch and back down to the boat, so we could simply untie one end and pull the rope free.

George on beach, Rio Tocantins, his diapers hanging off our masts

When we resumed our voyage a powerful oceanic tide started combining with the dam's rhythm, confusing us as to the schedule. In the riverside communities the boats were moored to tall poles set in the river bed. The streets were of bare dirt, the houses of stained planks. Special school boats, yellow like school buses, brought little students into the towns. On the docks were burlap bags full of acaí, an un-sweet fruit that looks like a purple grape. The locals boiled it into a pulp and consumed it in large quantities.

George entertains locals on the Rio Tocantins

Our last community on the Rio Tocantins was Baião. Here we experienced new heights of small-town hospitality. A woman we had met in São Paulo was from there. She had arranged for us to stay at her family home. Upon arrival we were to ask for her mother, Natalia. Everyone would know her, and it was easier than giving directions. We did so, and the people sent us to a certain house. However, unknown to the daughter, Baião now boasted two Natalias and this was the wrong one! No problem: Natalia number 2 gave us a ride to the home of Natalia number 1, a modest brick house near the port. This woman put us in a spare bedroom and immediately began serving us the famous foods of Pará. Knowing we were coming she had already started a big kettle of *maniçoba*. The head start was necessary because *maniçoba* takes a week to cook! The principal ingredient, cassava leaves, are poisonous otherwise. (It also includes salted pig's ear and beef tripe.) Also in Baião, while taking George for a walk I stopped at a bakery. The proprietors, a married couple, offered George and I some cold water. We appreciated that. Then they insisted on giving George a bath. Why not? And after taking him from the tub and drying him off they dressed him in a brand new suit of clothes! I never understood how they happened to have that on hand. When I brought George back to his mother she didn't recognize him at first!

The river grew steadily wider until it looked like we were entering the Atlantic, though the ocean was still a hundred miles away. Rather than exit the main stem of the Tocantins, on June 16th we entered a maze of islands and tidal rivers that provides a sheltered route to the city of Belém. In any given spot the current changed direction every six hours, but for us it might change whenever we reached a new intersection of waterways, because they branched and joined at odd angles. The hydraulics were complex and unforeseeable. We waited out periods of strong contrary current only to find it against us again at the next intersection. The land was low and swampy, the shore lined with shacks on stilts. The houses often had large boats propped up next to them; they had been moored there on a spring tide and could only leave at similarly high tide. Being unable for several days to go ashore and walk was a burden for little George, who, at fifteen months, was eager to exercise his wobbly little legs. He compensated by standing in the companionway and marching in place.

Everything moved by river. Each community's waterfront was a beehive of boats loaded with bricks or fish traps or people. One boat was transporting heavier-than-water logs. Several massive trunks, as long as the boat, were suspended from each side, at and below the waterline, parallel to the keel. Members running transversely across the gunwales supported the heavy ropes that looped down and cradled the logs.

The waterways became small, then big again as we approached Belém, at the southern margin of the vast Amazon delta. On June 19th we reached this city of 1.5 million inhabitants. Our final approach was across a mile-wide channel which was ebbing swiftly; we angled sharply into the current to cross. The skyline was a mass of high-rises while the waterfront was a chaotic succession of docks, sawmills, and boat yards.

Ginny had found reference on the internet to a yacht club. We found it, and were immediately welcomed. Their dock was unprotected, but we were soon hauled out on a trailer and deposited among dozens of other boats in a fenced area. Two other foreign vessels were present: a Swedish yacht skippered by a formidable single-hander named Eva, and a boat with a hard-drinking Russian couple. The latter had recently been robbed by pirates while anchored at a nearby island. "The joke was on them," said the man, Anton, "because our stuff was mostly broken!" Now they were waiting for a new starter motor so they could escape to Trinidad.

The trailer being rather tall, we scrounged old tires and boards to make steps up into the boat. Someone gave us a worn-out boat cover, which we stretched out between tall boats to either side for shade. To make more room in the boat we pitched our tent and put some of our stuff in it. The nights were cool but by noon it was oppressively hot. In the afternoon an intense storm usually hit, testing the web of ropes holding our tarps together and covering the ground with an inch of water. I finally broke down and bought a pair of flip-flops, the best footwear in the constant dampness. And this was the dry season!

One of our favorite memories of George takes place in this boat yard. We had taught him to walk by accompanying him on either side, each of us holding a hand. When he no longer needed us he still walked with his arms up in the air! He was also in the habit of carrying objects he found to be of interest. On the day in question he was seen stalking away from our camp toward the fence separating the boat yard from the city. In each upraised hand he brandishes a stick! His walk is an awkward clump. From behind he looks like a monster on his way to destroy the city except for a question of scale.

Ginny taught me how to use the software for mapping and photography. I also researched navigational problems, including the dreaded *pororoca,* bore in Enlish. These are true tidal waves, as opposed to earthquake-generated tsunamis. The *pororoca* is up to five meters tall. It terrorizes the Amazon delta in times of extreme tidal flux. I watched videos, taken from aircraft, in which waves smashed into jungly shores and ripped the trees up. Anybody caught in that would be lucky to survive. Fortunately it only reaches such extremes in February and March. It was now the opposite time of year.

Belém, founded in 1616, is densely built on a low peninsula. The slums outside the marina gates were tumultuous and fetid, lacking drainage and sanitation. Loudspeaker cars rambled past blasting commercial spiels. The city was dangerous on its waterfronts, cleaner and more prosperous inland. The Old City, fifteen minutes away by bus, was very beautiful. We ran errands, like looking for a hat for George or new bowls to eat out of. Nobody had epoxy so we conducted repairs with polyester resin. Ginny memorized the shops offering free shots of coffee and steered us accordingly. While we extracted these materials and information from the city it was preoccupied with something else. The World Cup was going on and Brazil was the host! Yellow-and-green bunting filled the streets. When Brazil was playing every house and business had its TV on. When Brazil scored a goal fireworks and horns instantly blasted all over the city!

The Brazilians use the word *saudade* (sow-dáw-jee) a lot. It means a longing for loved ones. They are a loving people, and it was a pleasure to be among them. The word now applied to me, because on July 17th Ginny and George flew to Los Angeles, where her mother lived. We always knew this day would come, because we couldn't sail the open sea with George. I planned to single-hand *Thurston* back to Florida as quickly as possible.

Bottom repairs, Belém, Brazil

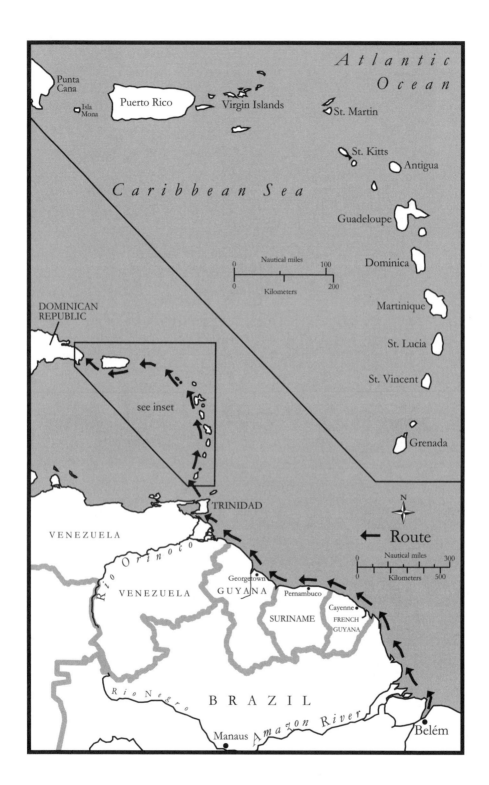

HOMEWARD,

Chapter 10

HOMEWARD, SOLO

With my wife and baby gone *Thurston* actually seemed roomy, but this was slim compensation. My job now was to rejoin them as quickly and as safely as possible, so I finished the boat work and mapped the Amazon delta by our usual method.

The delta extends 170 nautical miles from northwest to southeast. In this maze of islands, channels, and sandbanks nothing is much above or below sea level. Fifty miles out to sea the water is still only ten meters deep! The large tidal range creates powerful currents, the floods just as strong as the ebbs. And those *pororocas* can strike. Belém is on the Pará River: a short, wide collector of several rivers. Its mouth is seventy miles northeast of Belém. Tidewater back-channels connect it to the Amazon, which lies to the northwest. Thus the Pará and Amazon have separate mouths but share one delta.

My initial plan was to travel inland via the back-channels then exit via the Amazon's northernmost mouth. That way I would stay in rivers as long as possible and delay entering the Atlantic. But I changed my plans upon talking with my Russian friends, Anton and Julia.

Their boat was the *Scalawag*, a 37-foot Irwin cutter, built in the U.S. in 1976. They had already tried twice to exit the Pará mouth. Both times they were defeated by engine problems and strong currents. The second time they were cleaned out by pirates as well. "They came aboard at night, held us up at gunpoint, and took everything, even our clothes!" they said. But they were ready to try again, this time at the half moon, when the tides are in neap and the currents are slower.

I liked the idea of catching the next neap, just three days away, but the dangerous segment from the last anchorage out to the ten-meter depth contour was too long to sail between sleeps, so I asked if they could tow me. They agreed, and on August 6 the *Scalawag* towed *Thurston* out into the Pará River.

We were still within sight of Belém when the *Scalawag* lurched to a halt. The chart showed a depth of two meters yet we had ran aground. The tide was falling. By noon she was high and dry on a ribbon of sand, near where pirates had attacked them before. Anxious to free ourselves promptly upon the rising tide we set out anchors and dug a pit to facilitate turning the keel. As the water came up Anton and I winched her bow around to face deep water. Finally she lifted and we motored off.

Scalawag aground

Just offshore from where solid land ended we waited for the tide to change again. A three-knot current pulled the anchor chain straight as a rod. During the wave-tossed night a new sound brought us up on deck: a fishing net had gotten draped over the chain! A boat came close. Grumbling, mumbling men freed it in the black night. We went back to bed.

The next day favorable currents helped us sail past the critical zone, where navigable channels alternate with shoals where surf breaks at low tide. When we reached the ten-meter contour we turned northwest toward French Guiana. The sea was too rough for the *Scalawag* and *Thurston* to separate so we continued together through a third night.

I had slept during the day, so at 9:00 p.m. I took the helm. I sailed *Scalawag* through fleet after fleet of fishing boats, knowing each had a net several kilometers long that could catch on a hull appendage. Whenever I thought I had passed the last boat more lights appeared on the horizon. Innumerable small wooden vessels were working the shallows fifty miles from land, each a threatening point of light.

At 3:00 a.m. beautiful Julia came on deck. She and Anton often quarreled. I'd never had a conversation with her because she spoke nothing but Russian. The wind and sea were high. To make sure she understood the danger I pointed to one light after another, each time saying "Fishing boat," until I had completed a circle. "Fishing boat, fishing boat, fishing boat! Too many fishing boats!" I had dowsed the jib to slow the boat down. Julia indicated we should put it back up. We got Anton up to referee. They started bickering. Suddenly *Scalawag* went dead in the water. She had snagged a net.

A long net is the ultimate sea anchor. It doesn't move an inch relative to the water, whereas *Scalawag* and *Thurston* wanted to be blown downwind. The net slipped free of *Scalawag's* hull only to drape over the tow line connecting the two boats. Now the net was upwind and the boats were downwind, side-by-side, draping over the tow rope. I swam to *Thurston* and untied the tow line, hoping Anton could pull it through from his end, but it was stuck. Among much confusion of lines I sat on *Thurston's* bow and pulled hand-over-hand until I reached the net. The strain had caused it to snarl around the tow line. The best I could do was cut the line on either side of the snarl. It was my main anchor rode, detached from my anchor for towing purposes. I saved the two halves and would rejoin them later.

By this time it was nearly dawn. The wind had dropped. It was a good time to separate. I got my things and departed, anxious to preclude further calamities. By the time I got *Thurston* in order and raised her masts *Scalawag* had disappeared over the horizon.

The downside to having exited via the Pará mouth was that I now had 250 miles to travel before I would find safe refuge, much further than any previous passage. I would spend three nights adrift, difficult in *Thurston* because she rocks so violently, and I was already short on sleep.

The wind soon built to twenty knots from the east, an ideal angle. I flew all day, deeply reefed, the waves hissing as they slowly overtook me. At sunset I dropped my sea anchor, a cloth parachute attached to the bow by a stout line. The GPS now showed that a current was pulling me west at five knots. This speed and direction varied during the night as the tidal waters swirled. The wind never let up. *Thurston* oscillated once per second, sometimes to such an angle that her gunwales dipped underwater, obliging me to leave the cockpit drain open. Lying longitudinally was impossible so I curled up perpendicular to the keel in a fetal position. Better to be rocked in a berserk rocking chair than to be rolled back and forth like a log in the surf!

The next day I averaged six knots through alternating tracts of green ocean water and brown river water. Still fifty miles offshore, I steered northwest by the compass. Suddenly the GPS said I was going east though I was still headed northwest. Could a current possibly be so strong as to reverse me like that? No matter how I steered the GPS still said I was speeding east. A half hour later this anomaly disappeared and I was going northwest again. There was never any sense of acceleration or deceleration, but there never is in ocean current. Had the GPS allowed me to perceive a freak super-current, or had it malfunctioned for a half hour?

On the second night the sea anchor dragged me over a shoal only five meters deep. The wind blowing against the current created short, steep waves, like in a fast river flowing into a strong wind. This seemed dangerous as well as uncomfortable, so at 9:00 p.m. I got back underway. When I regained the ten-meter contour I hove to (main down, mizzen taut) and dozed in the cockpit for a couple of hours. Then some fishing boats got too close so I resumed sailing.

On Day Three I saw no boats. I fought drowsiness by singing songs. I heard voices, but knew they were from dreams I couldn't entirely suppress. At times I was able to adjust the sheets and tiller to make *Thurston* self-steer, and got some blessed shut-eye. This was fortunate, because my third night at sea anchor was also nearly sleepless.

On Day Four I was desperate to reach the shelter of Cabo Cassiporé. When the wind lightened I motor-sailed. When the sun passed its zenith I was able to escape its broiling rays by sitting in the shadow of the mizzen. Low jungle now appeared to port. I passed schools of large, silver fish that swam packed together on the surface, their gaping mouths wide open, evidently ingesting water. They bashed against my boat, seemingly insensitive to their surroundings.

When I finally reached the cape, scores of scarlet ibises and pink flamingos took flight from a wall of iridescent green trees. Behind the cape I tied to a snag near shore. There was no real land, just sea-level swamp and mud flats. The ebbing tide laid *Thurston* down in bottomless muck, but by morning she had refloated. High tide at sunset is a blessing because you will have it again at dawn, when you want to leave. Low tide at sunset means you have to anchor further out, unprotected.

On my final day in the Amazon's waning grip I rounded Cabo Orange. I stayed two miles from land but it wasn't far enough. I kept encountering depths of only a few inches underlain by muck. The water was so muddy, and the mud so watery, there wasn't much difference between them! These ragged capes are merely dumping grounds for the imponderable volume of silt coming out of the Amazon.

Rounding Cabo Orange I left Brazil and entered French Guiana. In a small river mouth I found the village of Ouanary. It was a speck of civilization in the jungle. From the boat landing a lane adorned with street lights and flowering shrubs ran to the high ground on which the village sat. Black women in colorful, flowing garb greeted me with *"Bonjour!"* There were no cars, just a few quads running on paved tracks. The school teacher, a huge man with a booming laugh, sat me at his computer so I could email Ginny. "I'm okay," I said. "I'm out of the mouth, in French Guiana. It's really cool here!" I washed my clothes, and spliced back together the anchor line I had cut to free *Thurston* from the fishing net in the mouth of the Amazon. The teacher's TV played the news from Paris. French Guiana is part of France just as Hawaii is part of the United States. The people spoke French Creole, and to a lesser extent French. Everyone had decent homes and enjoyed generous welfare benefits. My friend said that Brazilians mined gold in the local rivers and that they came into Ouanary for government assistance. This was illegal but tolerated. I hiked to the top of a small mountain. The view was of endless forest.

From east to west the Guyanas are French Guiana (a department of France), Suriname (formerly Dutch Guyana), and Guyana (formerly British Guyana). All have low, swampy coasts, heavily laden with Amazonian mud. The heat is oppressive, the tidal range is high, and the only harbors are a series of river mouths, spaced too far apart for small-boat convenience. These factors were against me, but the easterly trade winds and the Guyana Current would favor me as I sailed west.

I next sailed to Cayenne, the capital. Here I harbored in a narrow slough filled with fishing boats from Brazil, Guyana, and Venezuela. They were all busy selling their catch, refitting, and re-provisioning, conducting business in half a dozen languages.

With canoes in Cayenne, French Guiana

HOMEWARD,

The town was full of Gallic charm, with two- and three-story wooden buildings in a colonial style. On top of the hill was an old fort with a plaque telling how the valiant French had repelled a Dutch invasion in 1647.

I stopped at the former penal colony at Devil's Island but was promptly shooed away. An Ariane rocket was due to blast off that evening from the nearby Guyana Space Center, where Europe does its launching. In case their rockets have to self-destruct they clear all vessels from the area. So I proceeded to the Maroni River, boundary between French Guiana and Suriname.

On the French side was St. Laurent du Maroni, a tidy town teeming with French tourists. Here I made a new holder for my GPS, the previous one having broken. It's purpose was to hold the GPS at eye level on the mizzen mast, just forward of the steering station.

Albina, on the Suriname side, was very different. The people presented a confusing mix! They mostly spoke a Creole tongue called Talkie Talkie, but many also spoke Dutch, English, or French. Many were of East Indian or Indonesian heritage, descendents of indentured laborers. Aggressive black hustlers ran the cross-river ferries, a throng of wooden gondolas thirty to forty feet long, powered by two-stroke outboards. Many of these wore dreadlocks and the Rastafarian colors: green, red, and gold. The Chinese storekeepers kept aloof, interacting with their customers as little as possible while watching Chinese television all day. Brazilian gold miners worked the rivers in *garimpeiro* boats. Maroons also came into town. These were descendants of escaped African slaves who had formed hidden settlements in the bush. Each Maroon community has its own language! These people didn't all get along. In 2009 race riots had resulted in at least seven deaths in Albina. The spark was apparently an altercation between Maroons and Brazilians.

From the Maroni to the Suriname River was a hundred nautical miles. An energy drink kept me awake through the night while a half-moon boosted my confidence by illuminating the waves and horizon. I stopped a few miles inside the mouth of the Suriname River and got permission to tie up at a rickety dock. Crossing a mangrove fringe via planks on pilings I entered the village of Nieuw Amsterdam. The land was below sea level, diked and drained. The lanes were wide apart and paved with bricks. It looked much like Holland except the inhabitants were brown or black. At a cyber café I studied the geography in Google Maps and noticed a perfect five-pointed star on a nearby point of land. I went and explored it. It was the moat of a fort built by the Dutch in the sixteenth century! It still had cannons of several vintages, including some that were used to sink a German ship when it entered the river in World War II. On the other side of the river was Paramaribo, the capital. The city center was of ornate wooden buildings in an old Dutch style.

On the Berbice River, Guyana.
Hard to tell where mud ends and muddy water begins.

Sometimes I could reach the next river mouth in a day-sail. Other times I had to leave before dawn or sail overnight. It is unsafe to arrive at a new place in the dark but okay to leave in the dark if you have familiarized yourself with the route leading out to sea. The river mouths are deep and north-facing, free of breakers, but they contain hundreds of pilings that the fishermen have set to hold nets. Even miles from

206 HOMEWARD,

land there are long lines of hazardous poles to be avoided. And woe to anyone who should shipwreck along that coast because there is no solid ground, just uninhabitable mangrove. At spring high tides the sea covers the trees' roots. At low tide the forest is a morass of mud and pungent greenery.

I experienced this ecosystem one evening. I was tired of rough water at night, so I went up a tidal creek feeding into the Coppename River. When it became too small to go any further I tied to a branch. It didn't work out. No-see-ums kept getting into the cabin despite my fine-mesh net. Their bites gave me itchy welts. It was hot and stuffy inside, and the mangrove gave off a sour smell. As the tide fell I had to go out and loosen the lines. When the current switched direction I had to re-situate *Thurston* to stream properly in the center of the creek. As the tide rose I had to clear her of projecting branches that were trapping her downward. Each time I got out of bed more no-see-ums came into the cabin. A horrible night!

On September 8th I entered Guyana. Georgetown, on the Demerara River, did not appeal to me. The waterfront was all broken-down wharves. A young man frantically beckoned. He looked unsavory, but I needed a mooring. He tied my line to a dock composed of sagging beams then promptly requested payment for his services. He also warned that my boat might be stripped unless I hired him to watch it. Just then a police boat pulled alongside. One officer told me to climb up onto the dock. As soon as I got up there another officer boarded *Thurston* and ordered me to come back aboard. They asked questions and looked blankly at my papers. Finally they told me to report myself at the Customs and Harbormaster offices, a couple of docks back downstream.

I was leery because I hadn't cleared into the country, or into Suriname or French Guiana for that matter. I'd always been diligent about paperwork in my three-year voyage, and in my travels with Ginny. But on my own, with so many small countries to transit as quickly as possible, it no longer seemed worth the effort unless I planned to stay awhile.

At the Customs office they discussed whether I would need to hire an agent to prepare my arrival and departure documents. We had already experienced such wastes of money in Colombia and Venezuela.

"Tell you what, I'm leaving early in the morning," I said. "I just stopped here to get some sleep." The harbormaster finally allowed me to tie alongside a patrol boat provided I didn't go ashore. I left at dawn without paying anybody anything.

It wasn't far to the Essequibo, a larger river with islands in its delta. The coastline here was lined with buildings, the interior having been drained for cultivating rice and sugar cane. Every few miles I passed a canal opening with a tide gate for letting water out but not in. A few miles up I found a marina that had been recommended to me by Peter and Louise, the yachties Ginny and I had met on the Rio Negro. The owner was of Portuguese extraction and a former seaman. He was interested in my stories, and in telling his own. He had no dockage, just a ramp and sheds full of boats, so he pulled me out on a spare trailer.

The town of Parika was two miles away. It was there that I got word that my father had died. Ginny and George had been living with Mom and Dad. I was grateful to her for helping out during Dad's decline. My absence wasn't right, but I felt I owed something to the voyage, to finish it properly.

I went back to Georgetown by minibus to run an errand. The person sitting next to me explained that the political parties are based on ethnic divides. "The blacks can't run the country," he said. "The Indians can, but they're sons of bitches!" And I found that the Indians (meaning their ancestors came from the Indian subcontinent), whom I had imagined were one people, are split into Hindus and Muslims. In all three Guyanas the closer I looked the more schisms I perceived. The ethnic groups are small, the overall populations are small, and the population densities are small, but the diversity is sky-high.

On Sept. 19 I sailed to the Pomeroon River, another uninhabited mangrove bay. From there I had planned to travel by interior streams into Venezuela, maybe visiting Jonestown, which wasn't far out of the way. But by 3:00 a.m. I was so tired of mud, bugs, and tides I had changed my mind, and went back out to sea.

Twenty miles out a storm started gaining on me from behind. It was enormous, full of violent black energy. To get out of its path I steered further seaward, sped by the faster winds that radiated from it. The waves became brusque. A gust broke loose a vang fitting, causing my mainsail to flog. I jury-rigged it with a shackle and a piece of rope.

HOMEWARD,

When night fell I felt very alone. I still wasn't at home in the open sea. This time there was no moon. As the hours dragged by I fought the urge to look at my watch. Using a headlamp with a red light to avoid spoiling my night vision I constantly checked my GPS and steered to keep its red arrow vertical. (When navigating to a waypoint it gives you an arrow which rotates left or right if you go off course.) Fortunately the waves became regular and the wind died down to a steady ten knots from directly astern, allowing me to put one sail to starboard, the other to port, and set the tiller tamer to hold course. I buckled into my harness, slumped against the lazarette, and slipped into and out of sleep.

Around midnight I saw a brilliant light far ahead. I slowly gained on it, then skirted to one side. It was a big fishing boat, traveling my direction, busy at its work. I saw men on deck but they never saw me. Things like that make you feel lonely, but very alive too. Long solo passages are intensely emotional. Being cooped up with yourself forces you to think about who you are, what you're doing, and why. Arguably I didn't need this; I'm plenty introspective without all this extra soul-searching. I missed Ginny and George. I questioned the wisdom of continuing alone but was also enthralled by the beauty of the under-taking. The trawler slowly fell behind. I stayed awake long after in case it had nets out.

When sailing west it is best to make landfall by early afternoon, before the sun drops low enough to blind you. On the Guyana coast the shoals and high tidal range further restricted safe landfalls. It is undesirable to arrive at low tide, because your destination may be nothing but mud, or on an ebb tide, because you'll have up to four knots of current on your nose. I'd hoped to shelter in the Waini River, on the Guyana/Venezuela border, but these factors didn't line up for that. Fortunately everything fell into place for Caño Guiniguina, a mouth halfway around the Orinoco's vast fan-shaped delta.

By the time I sighted land, thirty hours after leaving the Pomeroon River, the wind had almost disappeared. The wind waves were now only glittery wrinkles on the surface of majestic swells the shape of corrugated roofing, very rounded and regular, but moving, rolling, lift-ing me up and down.

Inside the opening I passed a couple of Indian huts made of

thatch. Further on I stopped at a raft consisting of plastic drums lashed together, anchored out in the middle of the estuary to escape bugs. Under a plastic tarp was a crude camp. I visited with the dozen men staying there, the crews of three open fishing boats. I gave them a big plastic buoy I had found during the passage, perhaps lost by that trawler. I also gave them a hundred bolivares, worth about five dollars, which I had left over from when we were in Venezuela. I wasn't going to need them. I also valued their good will since I wasn't checked into the country and wanted no problem with the authorities, should any be around. It was reassuring to have friends nearby as I dropped anchor and cooked a long-deferred meal.

Floating fishing camp, Caño Guiniguina, Venezuela

I was out of the Guyanas. The bottom was firm now. The Orinoco water was a glossy, translucent brown, unlike the opaque tan of the Amazon. The following night I took refuge behind Punta Pescador, where I had stopped in 1992 as well, and the next day I rounded the point into the Gulf of Paria. To my right were the beaches and palm trees of Trinidad. Two days later I was in Port of Spain, the capital.

HOMEWARD,

Peter and his lovely wife Louise lived near Port of Spain. They had arranged a free haul-out for *Thurston* next to their famous power yacht, the *Passagemaker*. Thank you, good friends, for helping me prepare for my next leg!

Trinidad is the first of the Antilles, a chain of lofty, emerald-green stepping stones leading from Venezuela toward Florida, 1700 nautical miles northwest. My mission was to enjoy the ride while striving to reunite with my family. In the blue-water crossings to come, ultra-light, keel-less *Thurston* would be ill-suited, but in the early nineties I had sailed the same route in an even smaller, lighter boat, so I had no qualms.

On October 13, my preparations finished, I motored west around the precipitous mountain range that caps Trinidad's north end like a broad-brimmed hat. Exiting the Dragon's Mouth, northern gate to the Gulf of Paria, *Thurston* re-entered the Caribbean after an absence of three years. The mud of the Amazon and Orinoco had all settled out. The sea was sparkling blue to pewter depending on sun and clouds. My next passage was to Grenada, eighty miles north. Through this wide gap and others the Guyana Current flows into the Caribbean at a rate equal to its outflow via the Gulf Stream. I would be crossing the stream at right angles. To jump off further upstream I travelled twenty miles east along Trinidad's north coast. To minimize adverse current I closely followed cliff faces and dipped into amphitheater bays. Cactus and palm trees grew on rocky shelves. Where a lofty spur jabbed north into the sea I followed the example of a local skiff and cut through a narrow fissure separating the main island from a tall, craggy sub-island. The vertical walls of this marine alley were ten meters apart. A heavy ground swell ran through the gap, hissing against the walls, reeling and tipping through the chasm. I stayed in the center so as not to scrape a granite face. It reminded me of a carnival ride I went on as a child where you walk down a long, revolving tube.

At midnight I left Trinidad for Grenada, the motor at half throttle. There was no wind. A half moon illuminated sea and clouds. Heat lightning played in the sky ahead. The sun came up, and I droned on. What a wonderful invention the outboard motor is! At 4:00 p.m. I entered Prickly Bay on the south coast and anchored among hundreds of yachts sitting out the hurricane season there.

In the morning I visited with a wraith-like French Canadian live-aboard. "I sell art to support myself, but I've only earned $30 in the past three months," he said. He was skinny as a rail. His feet were swollen from malnutrition. I gave him some potatoes. He ate them raw. "I don't believe in cooking," he said. "Eventually I won't eat food at all, or drink water. They aren't necessary if you feel your spirit correctly. I only fear that I may not always be correct in this feeling." His boat was a worthless hodgepodge. The bottom hadn't been scraped for ten years. He had taped and twined a framework of plastic pipes onto the bow of his dingy, like a projecting prow, and intended this evolving sculpture to become his new main boat, in a logic I couldn't fathom. He had made it all the way down from Montreal, but to keep going south made little sense. I wondered what would become of him, starving, hardly able to walk, with a boat that could barely move.

I stayed only a day or two each in Bequia, St. Vincent, St. Lucia, and Martinique. Everything seemed smaller and closer together than I remembered, but just as lovely. Getting from anchorage to shore without a dinghy in these high-rent districts was a challenge. Sometimes I stuffed my gear into a waterproof bag, swam in, and changed on the beach. Other times I found places where I could wade ashore unopposed.

In Rodney Bay, St. Lucia, I thought I'd hit the jackpot. Behind the marina, which is perhaps the largest and most affluent I'd ever seen, I found a line of low-value local boats where the basin adjoins the coastwise highway. Some of them were utilizing miniature "docks" that had been extended over the riprap at the edge of the highway. Their owners obviously weren't paying much, so I pulled in among them. But as I tied up a Rasta-ish dude approached. "What you doing coming into my marina without getting permission first?" he angrily demanded. If his little docks alongside a public right-of-way could be called a marina, the contrast between it and the real one next door couldn't have been greater. "And have you cleared in?" he further queried. I'd have contested his right to charge me, but he had me over a barrel there. I needed to avoid the authorities so I went back out and anchored in the bay.

On the west coast of Dominica I found the Layou River unchanged. Just as in 1992, it was just deep enough, and I and the available little boys were just strong enough, to pull my boat up a 200-yard-long natural spillway over the gravel beach to a limpid lagoon. "Tie up good, the river runs strong when she rains," said a local guy whom I joined on the bank for conversation.

"Did you clear in at Roseau?" he asked.

I waded back out into the water before answering. "I don't have to clear in because I'm not on land, see?"

He laughed. "Don't worry, I'm not a policeman." Hustlers hassled me in the towns of these poor islands, but here in the countryside my acquaintance left when he saw I was ready to retire. Nor did anyone bother me at daybreak when I tied a line to *Thurston's* bow and lowered her stern-first through the river's final rush, leaning back against her pull. Where fresh and salt water joined, in a chaos of conflicting wavelets, I got in and continued north.

At each island's north end I passed through a zone of unpredictable gusts before emerging again into the unobstructed trade winds. As I sailed around the curve of islands my course angled more downwind. I tethered myself in for the rough crossings, typically fifty miles wide. They were easier in *Thurston* than they had been in *Squeak,* which weighed only 250 pounds. I then motored up the island's lee. Most of these Lesser Antilles were old volcanoes, bulky enough to shade me from the harsh morning sun.

At Guadeloupe I left my 1992 route and went north to Antigua. During the crossing squall after squall plastered me. They were black cloud masses with grey tendrils, visible well in advance but mercurial. They often dissipated before hitting, or intensified, a flimsy veil becoming a pelting downpour. You never knew how much wind they held, so I reefed in advance. If that wasn't enough I removed the mainmast and laid it on deck. This facilitated weather-vaning into an unexpectedly fierce wind. "What can go wrong?" I asked myself, because as the wind crescendoed it was apt to break a weak link in my boat. Then a sail might go out of control until I found a bit of hardware or line to fix it.

At Antigua I stayed in Falmouth Harbour on the south shore. It was a haven for English ex-pats who had sailed there long ago and stayed, and a focal point for high-end yacht racing. Two weeks earlier Hurricane Gonzalo had passed through, catching everyone by surprise. Over a hundred boats had been lost there and at St. Barts and St. Martin. The satellite weather image now showed a similar formation, so they were prepping their boats for a repeat. I moved *Thurston* to the island's best hurricane hole, English Harbour. It had been regarded as such since 1647, according to a captain's letter of that date. The letter was on display at Nelson's Dockyard, an old British shipyard which has been restored as a national park. Horatio Nelson commanded the post for a while, thus its name. But no hurricane came.

From Antigua I sailed to St. Kitts, a sixty-mile crossing. At the capital, Basse-Terre, I found a fishermen's harbour behind a short jetty and passed a tranquil night. The following day being Sunday no internet could be found, so I continued, past Dutch Statia and Saba, then to St. Barthelemy, another French island. Gustavia, its principal town, was a showpiece of modern yet historically sensitive architecture. A low esplanade circled the tidy harbor. The boats' sterns were all tied to buoys, so no one swung. Their bows were belayed likewise, or to the sea wall. The roofs were red like tiles but of a modern sheet material. Development had crept up the amphitheater of hills, but the peaks were still green.

On November 4th I reached St. Martin, the north half of which is French, the south half Dutch. During the crossing *Thurston's* tubular mizzen mast step had cracked again. Also the outboard motor's clutch was slipping again. These repairs would take a while, so I entered the island's large lagoon, which also is divided between France and Holland. At the Lagoon Marina, on the Dutch side, a husky blonde man in his thirties noted my arrival. "You know what this boat reminds me of?" he asked an older man who turned out to be his father. "Remember that *really* little wooden boat that stayed here a long time ago?"

"Was it in January, 1993?" I interjected.

"That's about right."

"Did you used to have a big map on the wall showing hurricane tracks?"

"Yes."

"That was me!"

The blonde guy, Bernard, was only fourteen at the time but he remembered me! Back then he was the son of the owner, a Dutchman. Now he managed the marina but his mother and father were still with him. They dug up a photo of me sailing *Squeak*. The marina had changed entirely, but the same family still owned it. As in 1993 the boaters were from many countries: England, France, South Africa, Brazil, even Slovakia.

On San Martin with Bernard, who remembered me
from 1993, when he was fourteen years old

Dozens of boats lay wrecked along the shore, victims of Hurricane Gonzalo. Masts were broken off, topsides holed, stanchions bent. One live-aboard had drowned. The survivors described the mayhem. "The wind clocked around to the west and blew at a hundred knots for three solid hours," they said. Many boats dragged anchor, sweeping other boats along with them. They smashed into the bridge and beat against concrete docks until they sank. The roller-furling foresails all worked loose and tore into shreds. Some planned to fix their boats, others lacked the money.

Rather than stay at the marina I parked under a new bridge that crosses the lagoon in the vicinity of the extensive live-aboard anchorage.

Here I paid nothing and was sheltered from sun and rain. In the shallow water by the east abutment I tied bow and stern to overhead utility conduits. Then I went ashore, found a heavy plank, and propped it up so that it projected toward *Thurston* like a diving board. I weighted the landward end down with rocks. The plank allowed me to step ashore without getting wet, though the maneuver was awkward; I had to duck walk the board to avoid hitting my head on the bridge's massive concrete beams!

Moored under the bridge on San Martin, with a plank for getting ashore

Thus ensconced I broke out the old mast step, gouged out soggy plywood core material where the mast passes through the deck, and waited for the remaining wood to dry before installing a new tube. A modern supermarket lay ten minutes away. Another fifteen minutes along a congested road brought me to the Lagoon Marina, where the bar had two-for-one beers at Happy Hour. Rainstorms often flooded the streets. One occasionally heard Dutchmen conversing in their native tongue but mostly people spoke West-Indian English. Many had migrated there from other islands or from Guyana. On the bus the principal language was Spanish because the laborers were largely from the Dominican Republic.

Since leaving Belém I had averaged twenty miles per day including days in port. Such rapid progress was largely due to my route's favorable orientation to the trade winds. At this rate I would reach Florida in January. Ginny sent me pictures of George, and we Skyped on Mondays and Thursdays at 4:00 whenever possible. Next I would cross the Anegada Passage. Then the Virgin Islands, Puerto Rico, and Dominican Republic. If my luck held my final approach would be via the Turks and Caicos and the Bahamas. Our friend Larry Whited could probably be persuaded to meet me somewhere on the U.S. coast with *Thurston's* trailer.

At midnight on November 19th I began crossing the Anegada Passage, course 300°. As clouds flew west, windows of open sky flew with them, framing ever-changing patches of stars. *Thurston's* compass was unlit. I didn't want to ruin my night vision by keeping my headlamp lit, so I kept finding new stars to steer by, each with a different reference point on the boat, like the motor's gas cap or the starboard oarlock. I changed star and reference point every ten minutes or so. The lights of St. Martin and Anguilla dulled and faded astern as the night progressed. The wind blew at ten to twenty knots.

In the morning a series of rainstorms passed. Before they reached me I rolled up the mainsail and sailed by mizzen alone in case they contained squalls like those that had pummeled me in the Guyanas. This precaution proved unnecessary because the wind hardly varied as they passed over. I was no longer in the tropics; the cool, damp air allowed me to wear rain pants and a windbreaker without over-heating. I set the main ninety degrees to starboard and the mizzen ninety degrees to port, and sat on the port side. This balanced the boat and faced me somewhat more aft so I could see oncoming waves better. They were six to eight feet tall, worth keeping track of. To stay awake I drank a 1.5-liter bottle of cola. All day I saw only one vessel, a cruise ship stalking the world's rim like a huge, white ghost.

Virgin Gorda (Fat Virgin) is a smooth, nicely rounded mass of mountain. Haze hid her until she was only sixteen miles away. This stressed me somewhat but not nearly as badly as in 1993, when I had no GPS and almost missed the British Virgin Islands altogether!

The sparkling white sails of chartered sailboats flitted here and there as I cruised downwind through the Virgins, spending nights in Tortola, St. Thomas, and Culebra. In towns where waterfront was expensive and there was no public landing I looked for a place where I could step ashore without opposition yet that was public enough to deter thieves. It was usually in a quiet corner near a public road.

The water along the south coast of Puerto Rico was brilliant blue where deep, jade green where shallow. I reefed to avoid surfing, averaging 5.5 knots. Going faster was too stressful. Wing-on-wing is *Thurston's* usual downwind mode, but I sometimes kept both sails on the same side, allowing the mizzen to partly blanket the main. In effect this is another form of reefing, and with both sails on the same side I could heave to (sheet the mizzen in and point to windward) without having to jibe either sail.

Ponce is the principal city on the south coast. As in 1993 I asked the Ponce Yacht Club management if I could anchor off their beach and access town through their gate. This time they weren't so enthusiastic. But I had a secret weapon. In case their response should be negative I had brought a copy of *Three Years in a 12-Foot Boat* ashore with me. Opening it to page 342 I showed them the paragraph describing their warm hospitality on that occasion. Honoring that precedent, they changed their minds.

I now had a safe base of operations. As in 1993 I walked a lot because the stores are miles inland. I even found white gas at the same Kmart! This was a great relief after using automotive gas in our stove for three years. Puerto Rico feels comfortable to an American because the people there have a sort of dual identity, half of which is fellow American.

From Boquerón, at Puerto Rico's southwest corner, I sailed halfway across the Mona Passage to Isla Mona. It stands by itself, a five-mile-diameter pancake of land. There is no good anchorage so I went around to the lee side and squeezed in past a scattering of coral heads and double-anchored near the beach. In 1993 I hadn't lingered there because a cold front was imminent. This time I stayed a second night. It was a nature reserve, with only a small staff and sportsmen that came to hunt the wild goats and pigs that impact the native sea turtles and the Mona iguana, which exists no where else in the world. I hiked all day on trails etched through the cactus and small-leaf scrub. The island is a plateau surrounded by cliffs. It is made of karst, a crackling limestone full of caves and sinkholes. Only at the end of the day, my feet satisfactorily blistered, did a ranger tell me I wasn't allowed there because I didn't have a permit.

*On Isla Mona I left my clothes on this bush overnight,
ready for another hike in the morning.*

The second half of the Mona Passage concerned me more. In 1993 I had sailed around the south side of Hispaniola (the island that is half Dominican Republic and half Haiti), immediately enjoying the protection of a southward-projecting cape. This time I wanted to go north-around to position myself for the Turks and Caicos. The capes on the east coast of the Dominican Republic project eastward into the wind, providing no protection. I pinned my hopes on a series of spots I had identified with Google Earth where a small, shallow-draft boat might find refuge behind corals and mangrove, depending on sea state. My immediate goal was a lagoon at a place called Bávaro, just north of Cabo Engaño (Cape Cheat). The imagery showed boats anchored there and a breaker-less gap through the reef.

It was December 1, 2014. The sea outside Isla Mona's lee was fierce. As on only a couple of prior occasions, I left the cockpit drain open because I couldn't keep up with the bailing. With the drain open a few gallons of water ride along in the footwell, robbing *Thurston* of a bit of her buoyancy, but it doesn't get any worse. The swells were about ten feet tall. I steered northwest, and in the afternoon sighted a low coast to port. I rounded Cabo Engaño several miles out. Here the coral reef began, paralleling the coast a half mile out. The lagoon between reef and beach was exposed to wind but free of swell energy, it having been dissipated in huge breakers. I passed a skiff fishing outside the reef. It was visible only on rare moments when both it and *Thurston* were on top of a wave, a sure sign of deep troughs and tall crests. But there must be a way back in or the skiff wouldn't have come out.

Upon arrival at the pass per my GPS map I got another indication that I could enter: no white water was visible in the gap. Anchored boats lay just inside. I ached to be there too. To make sure I should have lingered outside watching. Big waves come in sets and the interval between sets can last five or ten minutes. But I was anxious to be done with it, so I reefed down and steered into the gap.

Everything looked fine until I was in line with the breakers to left and right, meaning I was crossing the reef itself. Suddenly a roar drew my attention. A breaker as tall as those on either side was rearing up behind me! I steered perpendicular to it but knew I would broach or somersault. It happened so quickly I captured no image of the capsize, nothing to "play back" later. I had time for a single, "Oh shit," then I was swirling underwater like a rag doll, blind and powerless, with no idea of up or down. My tether towed me waist-forward for a few seconds (it was clipped to my belt and fanny pack strap), then the belt and strap broke, freeing me. Suddenly I broke the surface. *Thurston* was back on her bottom. She had quickly self-righted because both masts had broken off. Masts, booms, sails, and oars were floating just upwind. The wind was blowing *Thurston* toward the beach faster than the flotsam.

220

We were past the breaking zone so I climbed aboard and dropped the anchor. (It and the rode had stayed in place under their cover at the bow.) We were in the zone of corals, however. In the wave troughs their orange, columnar heads rose almost to the surface; I saw them through the turbid, turquoise water. This wasn't much of a pass after all!

I swam this way and that recovering *Thurston's* floating parts as they drifted by. The masts hadn't simply come out of their sockets. They were broken. Each consisted of a smaller-diameter upper aluminum tube lodged inside a larger-diameter lower tube. The upper tubes had broken where they emerged from the lower tubes. The main sail had a hole in it. The mizzen was shredded. My precious sliding-seat rowing station had escaped its holder and sank. The motor had spent time underwater, so I didn't bother trying to start it. I was no longer in danger. Civilization lay a half mile downwind, across the lagoon. I could paddle there. But as I pulled the last piece of mast and sail aboard an open boat drew up.

Broken mast, Punta Cana, Dominican Republic

They were two Dominican Navy sailors come to tow me away. I tried to pull up the anchor but it had snagged on a coral head, so I tied a buoy to its rode for later retrieval. We connected our boats with a line. Afraid of further waves, the Navy guys quickly pulled away.

At the anchorage I dropped my remaining hook. The other boats were for the tourist trade: marlin-fishing boats, pseudo-pirate party barges, glass-bottom excursion boats, etc. *Thurston* had performed as designed. No water had entered the cabin. Her twenty-four tanks and bins, which ballast her, had shifted to starboard an inch or two, riding up and over the bumps that book-end them laterally, but they had not come loose. The floorboards, made of 3/16" aluminum, had bulged upward but their edges were still trapped under the port and starboard rails that held them down. I hammered everything back into place. Loose objects had travelled in circumferential paths. Evidently the breaker had slammed her starboard-side down then rolled her at least 360°. Her mast heads must have hit bottom on the way.

Satellite photos are a weak guide because they capture only a point in time. The white of breakers is clearly visible but one has no information as to swells, wind, or tide when the photo was taken. These factors may be more or less conducive to breakers when you arrive. In this case they were more conducive. I should have studied the pass more, cruising back and forth at a safe distance. I would have seen occasional breakers and known I had to keep to sea that night. Protected water is like the Sirens, in the Odyssey, who lure the sailor onto the rocks. He craves rest so much that he succumbs to wishful thinking and relaxes his vigilance.

I had capsized due to waves several times during my 1990-93 voyage, but never in one of these bone-crushers. I had always wondered what it would be like; now I knew. I lost the rig only because I was sailing at the time. If I had rolled up the sails, lowered the masts, and motored in, the sailing rig would have survived. If I had secured the rowing station better it would have survived too. Always new lessons.

I had to stay put in that rough anchorage for a day and two nights before officials came by boat and cleared me in. Then I anchored closer-in and swam ashore. I walked in both directions looking for items lost in the capsize, like my cockpit cushion or water bottle, but too much time had passed. Dozens of swarthy men in jump-suits were raking seaweed off the beach. The coast was a huge tourist complex! For twelve miles the beautiful beach is strung with fine hotels. Millions of vacationers visit annually from all over the world. They call it Punta Cana after another minor point. I suppose that name has a better connotation than Cabo Engaño.

I shipwrecked in a busy place

My immediate beach supported dozens of Dominican and Haitian workers. They were gift-shop hawkers, boat operators, and masseuses. One guy trained manta rays at a nearby aquarium. Another took people up in a flying boat. All day long they said, "Hello my friend!" to the people passing by in swim suits and tried to herd them this way or that. Inland there was no real town, just scattered commercial strips and malls.

My GPS had survived. I could tell by the track where the capsize had occurred, plus I had left that buoy on the end of my anchor line. So I borrowed a sit-on-top kayak and paddled out there. Unfortunately it was missing a plug and slowly filled with water, becoming more and more unmanageable. I made it to the vicinity but never saw the buoy. Everything looked different. There was no sign of a pass. I couldn't find the rowing station or anchor.

To fix *Thurston* would take time and money. Due to high tariffs and Byzantine regulations you can't easily import things into those countries. I didn't care to further delay my reunion with Ginny and George. *Thurston* had little market value. Better to sell her here for whatever I could get. But I paled at the thought of leaving *Thurston* behind after all our improvements. She was an extraordinarily successful boat.

Word of my situation spread. A mechanic fixed my motor for free. The clerk at a pharmacy gave me his wi-fi code. Most importantly, the landlady for a cluster of shops gave me a space under a stairway to sleep in. It was right on the beach, so I could keep my eye on *Thurston*. The floor was sand. The space was just big enough to lay down with my stuff stacked around me. A flimsy plywood door gave me privacy. Nobody suspected that someone would be sleeping there.

Where I slept in Punta Cana

HOMEWARD,

I let it be known that *Thurston* was for sale for $1000. A fishing-charter crewmember known as Tio immediately spoke up. He was of mixed African and Hindu blood, barrel-chested, with graying hair tied in a bun. His posture was erect, his face sharp, almost fierce. He got along with everyone yet kept aloof. Having lived in Brooklyn he spoke English, often finishing a statement with the words, "You know what I'm a-sayin'?" Dedicated to work and family, he also laughed a lot and appreciated a good adventure. He wanted to restore *Thurston* and keep her unchanged. He would use her personally, not as a tourism venture.

Tio, Thurston's new owner

It took a week for a lawyer to draw up the papers. Tio could only scrounge $700, which I accepted. Meanwhile a Naval Intelligence officer smelling strongly of corruption periodically reminded me to report to him before I left the country. His organization had already extracted twenty dollars from me when they searched *Thurston* for drugs, and they wanted another crack at me after I had received payment for the boat. Tio and I thwarted him by keeping my departure date a secret. I bought a ticket on-line but pretended to not know when I would be leaving.

It took several days to work out what to carry home on the plane and what to ship via DHL. Ginny and I had accumulated a lot of stuff considering how small *Thurston* was. I kept swimming out to her until only those things I would leave for Tio remained aboard. On my last trip I gave her a final look-over, then lingered. I sat on her bridge deck, my left arm and side resting against her cabin top. With my right hand I patted her starboard gunwale affectionately. I cried profusely. "You're a *fucking* good boat," I swore, "A *fucking* good boat!" And so she was. What other vessel could have taken us all those places? Her every detail was honed to perfection in the rough-and-tumble of shoestring voyaging. On her we'd seen the world and conceived our son. In sickness and in health she'd been our home and our vehicle. My bond to her was very strong. I couldn't conceive of a more beautiful boat, but as Ginny said over Skype, "It's time to let her go." We had used her relentlessly in many strange lands, and there is no better way to honor a boat than that.

On December 14, 2014, almost five years to the day after we departed from Pine Island, Florida, I hitchhiked to the Punta Cana Airport and caught a plane. Arriving at Sea-Tac Airport I quickly located Ginny and George. We group-hugged. My son stared at me, grinning, making sense of it. He was still only nineteen months old. For five of those months he had seen me only on Skype. Now I was Daddy in the flesh again. We drove to my family home in Bremerton, where they had been staying with my mom.

The next day I bicycled to our local Goodwill store and bought a belt. Then I threw away the rope I'd been using to hold my pants up since the capsize. I was no longer a shipwrecked sailor.

Reunion at Sea-Tac Airport, December 2014

Chapter 11
LESSONS LEARNED

Wanderlust, loneliness, and satisfaction

The other day I asked Ginny, "What did you learn on the voyage?" She was in the kitchen making sandwiches. She paused for a second then said, "I learned that cruising is a simpler lifestyle than the conventional one, better in many ways. But there's a cost. You lose touch with your friends and family. You make new friends all over the place but after you move on you usually lose touch with them, too." She meant, I think, that we lose touch with everyone *but ourselves*. Surely it is to get in touch with *something* that one travels.

Call our voyage "open-ended cruising." Our route evolved over time. We had no end date. This was Ginny's first open-ended journey and my third. When I was eighteen I hitchhiked and rode motorcycles for a year. When I was thirty-six I began my three years in a twelve-foot boat. When I was fifty-four Ginny and I commenced the travels which culminated in this five-year voyage. Eighteen, thirty-six, fifty-four: I have started a new open-ended travel every eighteen years. This may be a coincidence, but it wasn't by plan. And each time it has taken longer to get the wanderlust out of my system.

When we are young we are more impressionable. The experience quickly shocks us into new level of maturity. But as we grow older we build up a protective reserve. There is less in us to be changed. Though a later-in-life voyage may be just as intense, though we travel just as wholeheartedly in lands just as foreign, or in wilderness just as pure, it takes longer to affect us as deeply, to satisfy that same wanderlust.

That said, this voyage was different because I was with Ginny. I didn't get lonely like in my previous travels. Together we never lost our gusto. Having a baby prevented us from completing the voyage together, but our bond was never in danger.

On boats

I bought my first boat in college. It was a San Francisco Pelican, twelve feet long. *Squeak,* of the same length, was my answer to the Pelican's limitations: lighter, faster, and with a sealable cabin. *Thurston* provided the same level of accommodation per person as *Squeak* but there were two of us so she had to be nearly twice as big.

Quantifying boat work is tricky. There are three phases. First you build her, or buy and adapt her. This takes far longer than you anticipate. Second, you cruise while debugging and adding improvements to suit your new life-style. This phase took us two years. Then phase three begins: just on-going maintenance and repairs. Phase three requires less boat work, so you get big returns on your investment. Our advice to a prospective voyager is that you set yourself a realistic goal in phase one. Don't build unless you love building. Then make it all the way through phase two. Then stretch out phase three as long as possible to profit from your investment. Let it live while your wanderlust lives! Let it not taper off, but continue in spate until you return home exhausted with a proven boat. Then pass it on.

Cruising in a small boat

Thurston was twenty-one feet long, five feet wide, and nine inches deep in the water. To the stock boat we added a cabin top, drinking-water ballast, sliding-seat rowing, and stowage systems. How did that work out?

Shallow draft multiplies where you can go. It allows you to seek refuge in more places. It reduces the likelihood of damage because a rock close enough to the surface to hole your hull is usually visible, either in itself or in the wave action above the rock. You can generally ignore depth information on charts and those cruising-guide instructions for avoiding underwater hazards. Just go where you don't see rocks. Your boat's bottom should be fairly flat so you can take ground. Lee-boards and centerboards are equally forgiving but centerboards require a trunk in the middle of the cabin. A kick-up rudder is a must.

If you do hit something, light weight reduces the risk because there is less momentum, therefore less damage. When that wave threw us onto the dock in Venezuela the damage was worsened because two heavy-set government officials were aboard. Their weight increased the battering-ram effect. They were throwing their weight around in two senses at once! Light weight also lessens the amount of flotation needed to make her sink-proof.

Provided your boat has lots of sealed compartment volume, complete self-righting isn't necessary in a small boat. You will be there, leveraging your weight as necessary to right her. Practice capsizing, and keep your hatches shut! In an unballasted boat closed hatches allow you to right her. Beware large, non-bailing cockpits because if they fill, the boat might tip under that weight. In 1990 I capsized at night off the coast of Colombia when a rainstorm filled the cockpit while I was asleep in the cabin! In sum, I would rather keep my boat light and maintain hatch discipline (or have a multi-hull) than hang lead off the keel.

Which isn't to say *Squeak* and *Thurston* had no ballast. A live-aboard carries lots of water and other heavy things. Both vessels placed tankage and stowage on the cabin sole. Even with the boat upside down it stayed in place, helping me to right her. In *Squeak* it was stuff that had to be moved out of my sleeping space at night. In *Thurston* it was a four-inch-tall tankage/stowage system locked onto the floor.

Thurston was a small live-aboard for three people, one of whom was a grabby, crawly, pull-everything-down, incredibly endearing one-year-old son. Her internal volume was about the same as our Volvo station wagon. We had to contort ourselves and minutiously stow our gear. But it was worth it for the flexibility. We got close to nature, up the smallest creeks and into the shallowest coves. At a beach we nosed up alongside the local watercraft. She was sub-optimal offshore, but we survived many overnight passages and storms. Carefully sailed, *Thurston* offered adequate safety. She had no lifelines but we wore harnesses at night and when it was rough. We carried a sea anchor, a signaling mirror, and similar devices.

To state it negatively, *Thurston* was too small. It was hard for the rowing station and the non-rower to coexist in the cockpit. The cabin was cramped. We couldn't stock up on anything. I had to let my accordion go. We coped by making it a rule to put everything away relating to the prior activity before getting things out for the next activity. For example, if we had just filled water bottles and now planned to sew on a piece of Velcro, we put away the water tank and close up the floor boards before getting out the sewing kit. I was the "put-away Nazi." Ginny remained a spatial anarchist, but she is also a conciliator. That is, she always conceded, under protest.

But *Thurston* was also too big. We couldn't pull her up the beach by ourselves. She was too heavy to row fast and too long for the typical boat trailer in Brazil, where we portaged seven times.

She was equally too big and too small, therefore she was just the right size, until George came along. Then she was definitely too small!

Working the boat

In the absence of self-steering, twenty-five miles per day is a good average for active periods. Five or ten miles per day is more realistic overall.

A light boat is a flimsy platform on which to brave big seas. Understand her weaknesses, perfect her fittings, and arrange her details so that tasks can be accomplished quickly, preferably with one hand. Add a lashing here or a leverage there to facilitate the work. Foresee the extremes. What if you are struck by a squall so strong your usual reefing procedure is impossible? Can the boom trip in the water when sheeted way out? Up to what angle from the wind can you sail under bare poles? How would you steer if your rudder broke?

In a small sailboat you are constantly adjusting sail area to suit the wind. Safety and progress depend on doing this well. The smart sailor raises and furls his Dacron with the nonchalance of a sea gull spreading and folding his wings, patiently accepting the tedium.

Crossings

No matter how many crossings we had under our belts we still hated them. We detested the unrelenting motion, the sleep deprivation, the fear that comes from being far from land. We despised sailing on dark nights, unable to see the sails and waves. We suffered the cold and wet. But we always made it, and in retrospect they possess a terrible beauty, like flashes of lightning in the sea of our memories. To recall certain moments is to evoke a primal awe, like the time I awoke from a catnap on deck during our crossing from Cuba to the Yucatán, and found Ginny hissing like a snake with each exhale because she was steering in a state of sheer terror. She doubted her ability, but I believed in her.

Refuges

After the trial by wind and waves every cell in your body cries out for rest. Some coasts are blessed with refuges, others are barren and forbidding. In some respects a small boat has more options for getting out of the sea. It can squeeze into smaller spaces and clear more obstacles. In a breaking river bar, however, a larger boat has the advantage because it can withstand bigger waves, and a speedboat is better still because it can power in between crests.

The small-boat enthusiast would like to see a different data set from that offered in the cruising guides, like the location of small boat landings and information allowing prediction of breaker size. Satellite imagery partially fills the gap. We loaded Google Earth onto a laptop and used it to study upcoming shorelines when we had internet access. We looked for coves, lees, reef openings, and deep river mouths. For each refuge we created a GPS waypoint and a spreadsheet record with columns for rating (good or maybe), type (bay, river mouth, or island), distance from known points, and compass directions from which the spot is exposed. In the South American rivers we gave up on finding charts and got into the habit of making our own. Using Google Earth's art tools we traced the shorelines and noted important features like towns and road accesses.

The Sea Pearl rolls uncomfortably in even mildly agitated water, making sleep difficult. It helped to keep her bow straight into the waves. Boats rarely do this by anchor alone; they all "water-ski" back and forth. If we expected the wave direction to remain constant during the night we lined up a stern line behind us and pulled the two lines taut. The fixed objects might be anchors, pilings, or trees. Where going ashore was feasible we often "perpendicular parked" close enough to wade ashore from the bow. Other times we anchored parallel to shore with a side line to a tree, and enough slack to pull the boat close and step off.

Docks present endless challenges. In the third world most are dilapidated or too tall. They tend to consist of horizontal structures when what you need is a vertical surface, like a piling, so your gunwale doesn't catch as you bob up and down. When our little fender got stolen in Guatemala we didn't replace it because it never helped. Two common-sense solutions come to mind. One, to protect her from the dock set an anchor out sideways. This allows you to spring her away from the dock. Two, if there is an interior right angle in the docking layout, tie up diagonally in the corner so nothing hits but you can get off from bow or stern.

Twice we obtained inflatables but eventually sold them because they didn't warrant the space they took up. Perhaps that is the best definition of a small boat: one in which it makes most sense not to have a dinghy. There is a nice halfway measure in warm waters, though. Bring along something that can carry your clothes and purchases while swimming, but that can be deflated or folded up. It may be a waterproof duffel bag or an inflatable kiddy raft. They take up almost no space and may come in handy. We also carried a tent for those nights when the anchorage was too rough to sleep but wading to a tent site ashore was possible.

One thinks of cruising as navigating, but really you are stationary most of the time. You spend long hours at anchor, docked, or tied to a branch. You stop at night, and often pause during the day. When you reach port you re-provision, run errands, fix things, make friends, and let them show you around. In half-a-dozen harbors we lingered for over a month. Thus comfort while *not* navigating matters. In the tropics this means a good awning to protect you from sun and rain.

Bilge water

A flat bottom is great for shallow draft and sitting level "on the hard," but there is no sump for bilge water to collect. We got around this by storing everything in waterproof bins with several inches of freeboard, and by periodically removing everything and mopping up the accumulation. In such a system even small leaks are intolerable. We didn't have a bilge pump, and were lucky never to have needed one. We ran a risk there.

Exploring new worlds

In cruising one encounters new lands. The newness is an end in itself, a source of rejuvenation, so it would be wrong to complain. But it is ridiculously time-consuming! At each new port one asks oneself, "How should we tie up? How is the security? Where can I get a city map? Groceries? Drinking water? Laundry? Wi-fi?" You make friends and see the sights. Then it's time to go and start all over again someplace else. When you get back home you are amazed how convenient it is to live where you know your way around.

Traveling abroad requires a lot of logistics because specialized gear is unavailable in the boondocks. We tried to keep a spare GPS, laptop, camera, Kindle, and headlamp in reserve, also plenty of motor parts. Cruising in home waters is much simpler.

Oceans vs. rivers

Our voyage took us through ocean and rivers in equal measures. Oceans offer a broader field of exploration but are more difficult and harsh. River travel, in contrast, felt so safe we decided to have a baby, a first for both of us. In rivers there is little danger of capsize. While he played or napped in the cabin we could leave the hatch open and monitor him.

On rivers you see lots of wildlife. The water is fresh, so there's less corrosion. It's easier to bathe, wash up, and dry clothes. If you run out of drinking water you can always filter the pathogens from the river water. Tying to a snag or branch is easier than finding an anchorage along a coast. You'll probably have to motor upstream, but it's surprisingly economical. Once purists, we came to enjoy motoring slowly. When motoring upstream, stick close to the bank, where the current is less. At a constant throttle setting your GPS speed readout allows you to determine current speed, which is helpful in deciding how to position yourself laterally in the river. Portaging around dams and rapids may be easier than you think. If you're going upstream, reservoirs work in your favor because they stop the current.

Hot and cold

Cold is difficult in a low-freeboard boat because you're always getting splashed. Rain gear, sea boots, and dry suits take up a lot of room, and how do you store them when they are wet? We sailed south to avoid that complication, passing through the tropics on our way to Argentina, and passing through them again on our return trip. Small-boaters are also vulnerable to heat because they rarely have refrigeration, biminis, or wind-scoops. Our awning was our best friend. We often kept it up all day and removed it at sundown to maximize air at night. After a couple of short-lived models we ended up with a heavy vinyl cover with grommet attachments in all the right places. We also learned to rely on a low-wattage cabin fan.

Cooking

This and the following two headings started as sidebars of a practical nature in our articles for Small Craft Advisor magazine during the voyage. The first explains how we organized our food and cooking.

Thurston's "galley" consisted of tools and supplies stored in various locations. To the right in the following photo is our MSR Dragonfly white gas stove in its home-made aluminum box. The box holds heat and blocks drafts. In the middle are our nesting pot, frying pan, and 1.5-liter pressure cooker. These all fit in the aluminum box on top of the stove. To left are plastic bins holding utensils.

At bottom is one of our water tanks. We usually either bought bottled water or filled from a municipal tap. Our water also served as ballast, another reason to top up frequently.

Not shown include a wooden bucket which held tall things like olive oil and vinegar, a large bin holding snacks, and a miniature hammock under the starboard side deck for fruits and vegetables. Under the floorboards were bins for grains, flour, noodles, and canned goods.

We had no refrigeration, so the first step in meal preparation was to check what needs to be eaten. Cooking and washing took place in the cockpit.

Repairs

Whether working in the cockpit or under a shade tree, I drew upon resources that I had found to be worth the space they took up. This photo, from top to bottom, shows *Thurston's* bins for:

· Boat parts (spare oarlocks, drain-plug, etc.)

· Motor parts (spark plugs, gaskets, etc.)

· Bolts, cleats & clips, eye straps & electrical bits, hinges & hose clamps, miscellaneous, nails, O-rings, pulleys & shackles, screws, and wire & washers, in alphabetical order from left to right, separated by dividers

· Grasping and measuring tools (screwdrivers, pliers, vise grips, crescent wrench, socket wrench, measuring tape, calipers, level, C-clamps, hammer)

· Cutting tools (collapsible saw, plane, files, rasp, punch, scissors, hand drill, bits, steel brush, knives, chisel, sharpener). Some of these are in a roll-up pouch to keep them sharp.

The large bin on the left contains fiberglass cloth and plywood bits. The one on the right contains brushes, mixing bowls, fillers, syringes, rags, and various adhesives. Not shown is a forepeak bin containing epoxy, acetone, paint, and thinner.

Some repairs necessitated borrowing something, like a vise or power tool. You can't bring everything.

Health

Thurston's medical stores emphasized prevention. Mosquitoes carry many diseases, so we had two nets for the companionway. The wide-mesh one in the lower left of the photo allowed more air to pass, which is important in the tropics. The one on the right has a finer weave for no-see-ums. The nets have elastic bands which snap around a lip on the hatchway for fast, secure installation. Between the nets you see a mosquito coil inside a round metal holder. A burning coil clears an area of mosquitoes, and the holder prevents burn damage.

The upper-right item is a pump-action water purifier for when there isn't a trustworthy water source.

Elsewhere in the photo are sun-block, insect repellant, hydrocortisone to relieve itching, first-aid items, and common internal medicines like pain killers and electrolytes for rehydration. Anti-histamines are useful against jellyfish and bee stings. In remote areas a course of general-purpose antibiotics may be advisable. Metronidazole treats giardia and amoebas.

Thurston had no bimini, so skin protection was crucial. My first line of defense was full-coverage light-colored clothing and hat. Sunblock protected the remaining patches of skin. I often needed to use an anti-fungal cream.

Cruising is a healthy life-style, and standards of hygiene have improved in Latin America. But in case something went wrong we carried a copy of *Where There Is No Doctor,* visible in the lower center of the photo. It tells how to treat yourself and those around you for a host of common maladies. It even tells how to deliver a baby! That was a possibility for a while, should George have come prematurely.

Closure

Our voyage met its Waterloo when I tried to get behind a coral reef in the Dominican Republic. A huge breaker rolled me because I forgot to wait for a larger-than-usual set of waves to come and go. I called it my Big-Surf Sayonara.

Ginny and George were waiting for me back home. For her the voyage was already over. Her closure was good. I called her. She helped me accept the fact that the voyage was now over for me, too. It was hard to let *Thurston* go, but we'd had a good run. It was time to move on.

ABOUT STEVE and GINNY

Stephen Ladd is a retired city planner. He is also the author of *Three Years in a Twelve-Foot Boat*. Virginia Ladd is a computer expert and "exhausted mother." Both are native Washingtonians. Their children are George Iguassu, born during the voyage, and Nathaniel Bowie, born in 2016. The Ladds live in Bremerton, Washington. A new boat is under construction in the carport. Though quite different from *Squeak* or *Thurston,* it too is meant for minimalist voyaging, should such opportunity ever fall to us again.